STOLEN BUT NOT LOST

by
Janet Tombow

Dedication:

To my mother, Norma Ellen Wallace

How special to learn the truth!

CONTENTS

PROLOGUE

It was Friday night. The plane was taxiing to the gate at Los Angeles International Airport after a four-day business trip. I had an aisle seat; a colleague was in the window seat and another across the aisle.

As we reached the gate, the flight attendant was announcing: "Be careful of items in the overhead bins as they might have shifted during flight." Before she completed that sentence, the eager salesman in the row ahead of me leaped up and opened the bin above my seat. Out fell a heavy metal luggage rack, landing directly on top of my head! I saw stars immediately from the impact!

People were naturally concerned for my safety, but I dismissed the incident as an "unfortunate accident." Despite the on-setting headache, I deplaned with the other passengers.

*   *   *   *   *

Little did I realize on that night in 1992, what a life-changing event this would be. I had just started asking God what He wanted me to do with my life, praying He would give me the courage to share my love for Him with others. As usual, God was ready with the answer, but knew I wasn't ready to accept.

Through miracles set to unfold, my life was about to radically change.

Chapter 1

GETTING THE MESSAGE

*"Being confident of this very thing, that he who hath
begun a good work in you will perform it until
the day of Jesus Christ." Philippians 1:6*

Fifty-one weeks after the airplane accident, I received a call from my colleague asking, "How are your headaches doing?"

I had not gone to the doctor during this time as a follow up to the accident. Not wanting to cause the company any workman's compensation issues, I consequently had just been self-medicating with over-the-counter headache remedies. The manufacturers definitely didn't recommend the dosages I was taking, but I was trying to cope.

In answer to her question, I replied, "Actually, the headaches are getting worse and more frequent."

"Don't you think you should go to the doctor to see if there is something wrong?" she urged.

I finally admitted I needed to do that. Through the company's personnel department, a workman's compensation claim was opened for the airplane accident. This was the last week in which to file a claim for the insurance to cover any related medical costs.

I was referred promptly to a neurologist, who scheduled appropriate tests for any permanent damage that might be causing my migraine headaches and the increasing discomfort I was feeling. All tests came back negative. With medication prescribed, he attempted to control the pain and decrease my discomfort, but without much success. After several weeks, the neurologist referred me to a Christian Family Counselor who had "experience with techniques to control or minimize severe headache pain."

Counseling Begins ...

I showed up to my first appointment with Beverly, the Christian Family Counselor, with far less than an open-mind. I felt strongly that I didn't need any psychological counseling. That was only for "crazy" people and I just had headaches!

As I sat with my arms tightly folded across my body during that first meeting, my body language certainly told Beverly that I was not interested in sharing my life story with her. Still, she began to probe about things in my life that might help her diagnose any under-lying causes of the headaches. It didn't take many questions and answers to realize this new relationship between us was appointed to unearth several deeply imbedded issues. Those issues would be the actual root causes of my migraines.

It was by Divine appointment that I was having this conversation. A five-year healing process was about to commence. Secrets of my past were about to surface. Some truths would have to be faced that would cause gut-wrenching pain. Many tears would result, many pages of journaling, and many days and nights of self-analysis. Many prayers would be needed to see me through this painful period of my life. I would see God at work through Beverly's role in my life. This was just one of the miracles of change I was about to experience.

Beverly asked: "What is it that makes you mad?"

"People who abuse animals and kids," I was quick to reply.

"Do you have examples of either?" she inquired.

That opened a "Pandora's box" about my life. I had been an abused child.

The memories of my younger years are few, and through counseling, I would learn why.

Some Childhood Recollections ...

I recall the automobile trip from Ohio with my father and great-grandparents. At five years old, we ended up in Southern California, but I was too young to understand the reason for the trip. I don't remember any mention of my mother or why she wasn't with us at this point.

I called my great-grandparents "Grandma and Grandpa Tombow." My father's parents died long before I was born, so these were the only "grandparents" on the Tombow-side that I knew.

My mother's parents were still back in Ohio; I had called them "Grandma and Grandpa Banks." Although I don't remember these things, we had lived with them just before we left for California and they had loved me very much. Grandpa "Joe" Banks' name was actually the first word I uttered. I was in my playpen when he came in from working the night shift. As he walked by me into the kitchen, I yelled "Doe!" which apparently was as close as I could get to "Joe." He stopped and came back to hear it again, then went into the kitchen to get others to come hear it too. But when they returned, I just smiled and refused to say it again. (Stubborn little kid!) I don't recall any explanation of why we had to leave Grandma and Grandpa Banks behind as we moved to California.

Grandma and Grandpa Tombow took care of me while father went to work. We used to watch boxing, wrestling, and roller derby a lot on television. Grandma and Grandpa would get really excited about those events that later I would learn were staged! Guess this was a first glimpse of "not believing everything you see or hear!"

We played cards often. I remember learning to play Solitaire, Gin Rummy, Go Fish, and Old Maid. I also recall learning 52 Pick-Up … but only had to play it once! While watching the adults play Canasta, I can still recall seeing Grandpa chewing his tobacco and using an old coffee can as a spittoon! Yuck! It wasn't very pleasant to kiss him good night!

I had a special blanket to carry around and wouldn't get too far from it. Talk about a "security blanket!" I would watch it in the wash using the round window in front of the washing machine. Neighbors would remind me later that, when it was drying on the clothesline outside, I would stand next to it with my thumb in my mouth and cry. I was lonesome for my mother.

My father built me a backyard playhouse; I could escape there for my own space. It had a little working stove in it, table and chairs, and even a telephone hooked up to the house. Painted white outside, the inside was unfinished wood; windows were on both sides, one with a view of the house and the other of my father's workshop. I can picture it better than my own bedroom in the house. I don't remember what I did there for activities, just that I really enjoyed spending time in my playhouse.

We had two fruit trees in the backyard that I liked to climb. I don't remember ever having dolls, but I do remember climbing trees. An early stage of being a "tomboy," I think. To this day I spell my last name for people saying, "Tombow, like tomboy with a W."

A few pictures show me on my swing set, dressed in my cowgirl outfit, complete with a gun and holster! I even had one of those stick horses to ride on, tethered to the swing set. "Roy Rogers," "Hopalong Cassidy," and "The Lone Ranger" were some of my favorite shows. I must have been one of their biggest fans.

My black Cocker Spaniel's name was Blackie. He would stay in the backyard with me while I played outside.

The Painful Parts …

My father married my stepmother when I was 6 years old. My stepmother later told me there were two conditions of their marriage:

> First, she required father to move my great-grandparents out of the house before the marriage.
>
> Second, she immediately became the family disciplinarian. This is a mild label for a terrible time in my life.

It didn't seem I could do anything right. How I responded to a question had the wrong tone or was being too sarcastic. A task wouldn't be done to my stepmother's satisfaction or as she had instructed. For a long time I believed she had eyes in the back of her head because if I made a face at something she said, WHAM, I'd get a slap in the face before I knew what happened! If I cried for getting that slap across the face, I would get told to be quiet or she would "give me something to cry about" - which didn't make sense because I was already crying! If I made a face at that illogical statement, an additional slap could be expected.

Often, I would be sent to school in tears for something I did wrong before leaving the house. Not a great way to start the day, with her yelling at me out the front door as I'm walking to school. Just as frequently, I would dread returning home after school for fear of some additional punishment for what occurred earlier that day, or likely I would do something else that was unacceptable.

I recall vividly the hard face slaps and body punches.

The beatings were most memorable as she used two-inch thick mail order catalogs or hard-backed hymnbooks. I was forced to lie naked on the bed with my hands tied behind my back with a piece of rope. If I cried or resisted at all, the punishment was longer or worse. I didn't catalog shop for several decades; I'm surprised I don't mind singing out of hymnals today in church with the memories they carry!

There were hours spent being forced to stand naked in the kitchen corner, bent over from the waist. If I peed the floor, because she wouldn't let me go to the bathroom, I would get beaten and made fun of.

She used to physically stomp on me. During these beatings, I remember wishing she'd break one of my bones, so maybe father would know how she treated me and would do something to stop it. If there were any bruises, they must have been coverable by clothing, or else she explained that I did them to myself, because I don't recall father ever asking me about them.

Threatening to tell father about a punishment would only result in more violent punishment. The same was true when I would say "I'm going to tell my Mommy on you!" She would counter with, "Your mother didn't want you or love you, so don't think she will be able to help you!" I remember her telling me several times that my mother tried to kill me in a car accident, because she didn't want me. That's a frightening thought to a little kid. Another story relayed often was that my mother ran off with a big, fat, ugly guy, leaving me behind.

Between my stepmother continually telling me these things and punishing me frequently for saying I was "going to tell my Mommy" on her, I lost almost every memory of my mother. I didn't remember what she looked like. I didn't remember any good times we had. I didn't remember any of the five years I was with her. I didn't remember why she wasn't in my life anymore. When you are told so often that someone doesn't want you or love you, or tried to kill you, eventually you believe it.

My lost memories of my mother, and my early childhood are living proof of how impressionable a child can be, especially when the telling starts so young and punishments hurt so much for bringing up the past. Finally you learn to give up, so the beatings subside and the pain eases.

Verbal abuse never stopped either. Verbal abuse can be as hurtful, detrimental, and life changing as physical abuse. This was used constantly to control my thinking and behavior. Whatever I did was never right enough. I was criticized for being too self-confident, and yelled at for being a smart aleck or getting too "big headed."

No decisions were allowed on my own as independence was discouraged or forbidden. I had to ask permission to go anywhere or do anything, even whether I could turn on the TV, in my growing up years. These requests were met with frequent lectures on how I got to do things my stepmother was never able to do and about how she had to stay home all the time so why should I be allowed to go anywhere.

Guilt is a terrible handicap and easily suppresses freedom and independence. Being made to feel you owe someone, or should be grateful to them for taking care of you, is an unfair position for any child. I remember her often saying to me, "How can you do (or say) that, after all I've done for you?? Don't you realize that I raised you when your own mother didn't want you?? I deprived myself of so much for you! You are so ungrateful!"

A child cannot be expected to respond properly to this type of logic. You're led to feel guilty that you deprived the other person of so much, that the debt will never be repaid.

I remember using my allowance, when I was 6 years old, shortly after my father and stepmother were married, to buy my stepmother her very first birthday present from me. It was a yellow soap dish purchased from the school carnival. I didn't mean it to be viewed as a cheap gift. It was all I could afford. I just wanted to buy her a gift and was trying to be thoughtful. She woke me up in my bedroom early the next morning, after father left for work. She started yelling at me that I "should never have bought that piece of junk" for her and, "if that was as good as a gift could be, not to bother to give any gift!!" Instead of being appreciative of the fact that I used my allowance to buy her a present, she reacted this way. I was only six years old, but I never forgot that frightful lecture, that's for sure!

After that, I used to get nervous about any gift I picked out for her, wondering if I would get it thrown back in my face or if she would treat it with disgust as she did the first gift. This led to later problems of my spending more for gifts than I could afford, but I thought better to do that than have the gift rejected or despised by someone to whom I "owed so much."

Mealtimes became something to fear. At 6 or 7 years old, I had problems eating, which eventually was diagnosed as a physical problem. It was a bug in my digestive tract that was prohibiting my being able to eat properly. However, until that problem was diagnosed, I was forced to eat. To make room for my meal, I would often go to the bathroom and make myself vomit. I guess no one suspected nor cared. One breakfast, after father left for work, I didn't think I could finish my breakfast, but that was unacceptable. My nervousness made me throw up in my cereal bowl, but I was still forced to eat what was before me. My other choice was to go to the kitchen corner for hours of standing naked.

I was actually relieved that there was something wrong with me and glad too that it was fixable. But I did hope my father and stepmother felt badly about how they treated me at the table all of those meal times before the problem was diagnosed.

I'm not sure which punishment was worse and I am surprised that all my "parts" stayed in place as physical as her abuse was! One time, she knocked me off a stepstool in the kitchen and a little piece of my front tooth broke off. But I was told to tell my father that I fell, if he asked. I often got beaten for telling lies, such as why I was late coming home from playing with friends (I used to turn back my watch and say I wasn't late according to my watch. That excuse only worked once, by the way!), or she would ask if I had eaten all of my lunch at school (only to learn later that she used to call the principal to check up on my eating habits! I thought she was clairvoyant for a long time to know I had tossed out my green beans!) But if it wasn't acceptable for me to lie in these kind of situations and endure the punishment for lying, I couldn't understand why it was okay for her to lie to father, or tell me to do so, when I had broken this tooth by her making me fall down. Needless to say, I suffered from mixed signals along with everything else!

The naked punishments were most humiliating. I recall being locked out of the house naked in the front yard for not taking better care of my clothes or some other offense. I was embarrassed thinking the neighbors had seen me this way. Years later, a friend would comment to my stepmother on how well behaved I was. She was shocked to learn from my stepmother of the methods she used to cause the obedience. The friend told me, after my stepmother died, how proud of her results my stepmother was and how she had just laughed about the humiliation caused by her methods when questioned by the friend.

The years of frequent painful physical abuse eventually broke my spirit. I would not fight back as often. Later I would say, "I'm not sure if I feared God more or my stepmother!" Gradually, I let her be a very controlling factor in my life. Her dominance extended into my adult life and severe resentment built within me.

Father's Role ...

My father's influence seemed almost non-existent. He was silent about the opinions voiced by my stepmother, never countered or corrected them. Perhaps that too was a condition of their marriage. However, if he was even remotely aware of the kinds of punishments she inflicted on me, I sure could have used his rescue instead of silence. It's commendable that a father would work two jobs to provide for his family, but another of his responsibilities should be to protect his children from harm. My father did not do the latter for me.

I'm also not sure what father told my stepmother about my birth mother. So, I cannot vouch if my stepmother embellished the version that "she didn't want or love me" my whole life, or if that was what she had been told. Either way it was cruel. I know some friends and relatives had been told my birth mother was dead. So, lying about the facts seemed to be acceptable under certain situations. For certain though, father was never my rescuer from my abusive stepmother.

We were living in Duarte, California, near City of Hope. On several occasions, I was forced to pack my suitcase, because I "was a bad girl," and then was driven to City of Hope, where I was left crying on the curb by the side of the road. Father and my stepmother would drive away and leave me for a while to cry and repent. Embarrassingly, I grew up thinking City of Hope was a home for bad kids during my childhood years! Their driving away was again a cruel form of punishment, another kind of abandonment for me. Since my stepmother couldn't drive, I do know my father was aware of this punishment and did nothing to stop it. When relating the stories, my stepmother would laughingly say that I only packed toys in my suitcase. I didn't see anything funny about it, just more humiliation.

Dreaded Music Lessons ...

I played the accordion for 10 years, beginning at age six. My stepmother played the piano and organ. Hers was a "gift" talent; mine was a "learned" talent - my terminology for playing the accordion, as it did not come "naturally" for me. It was hard work. This left me open to more criticism from someone who found it easy to learn music.

While I apparently did become a good accordionist, my stepmother would never give me the encouragement needed, only criticism for any mistakes made. I was forced to practice one hour daily. If I made a mistake in a section of a song, she expected me to keep practicing that part until I got it right. If I didn't practice the song enough times, that wasn't acceptable. I hated to practice; I hated her criticism; eventually, I hated to play.

Somehow our limited budget allowed me to quit playing in high school. But it wasn't until my mid-twenties that she asked me why I quit.

"I wasn't good enough," I responded.

She quickly said, "Not true!"

I used to play duets at state fairs and at the local service organization gatherings, like the Masonic Lodge or American Legion dinners. I would also play solos at our Baptist church. And, unfortunately, whenever friends would come to the house I would get asked to play a song or two for them, for which I hated being put on the spot. In retrospect, playing the accordion in public did give me some stage presence or confidence. I also received encouragement and compliments from many in the various audiences. But the one person I played for, seeking approval, never gave that encouragement.

So reluctantly, I asked that person, "How come you never looked at me from the audience? I thought you were ashamed of me and any mistake I made."

Surprisingly she said, "I was too nervous for you! You were really good at it!"

"Why didn't you ever tell me I was good?" I bravely inquired.

She replied, "Because I didn't want you to get a big head about it!"

Consequently, my musical career never evolved! A little encouragement along the way would have made such a difference!

While I don't play anymore, and have forgotten most of what I learned, this 10-year experience did give me a great appreciation for various types of music that I had played, especially easy listening and Christian music. It also gave me appreciation for what a musician goes through to become an expert at what they do. Without encouragement, however, it is tough to make the sacrifices needed to do it well and be successful.

"Elephant Training"

Gradually, all the pain and negatives wear you down. I was like the circus elephant chained tightly to a specific spot when young, chained long enough so he wouldn't wander off when an adult. Eventually, he would just stand at the spot even without a chain.

According to my father and stepmother, conveyed as usual by my stepmother, "College was too costly for the family budget and a waste of time for a girl. All girls want from college is a husband." But she said I was "welcome to leave the house and never come back" if I wanted to fund college myself. This was a threat with too much risk for me to face at 17 years old, so I just stayed home and went to work.

I was required to pay room and board for living at home. So, one-half of my weekly take-home pay from my part-time job at Tastee Freeze during the last few months of high school went to my father and stepmother. A similar amount was due for room and board from every full-time job I held. They had given me a 1956 Pontiac for my high school graduation gift. (I named her "Aunt Miranda." It was better than some of the names my friends gave their cars!) But due to financial difficulties at our house, I made the payments on the car going forward. I also donated the small high school scholarship I had received for college tuition to my father and stepmother to help with the bills. At least I learned early to pay my way.

No one I dated was ever good enough or acceptable. The criticisms of dates included the guy "was never going to be successful" (not sure how they could judge that about a guy 18 or 19 years old!); or the date didn't treat my father and stepmother respectfully enough. Their approval was too important to me; if I couldn't gain it, marriage looked highly unlikely in my future. That was the only way acceptable, from my father's and stepmother's viewpoints, for a single girl to leave home. If you lived with a roommate, you were "up to no good" or raised their concern that others would view me as a lesbian.

If I wanted to go anywhere or do anything, I had to ask permission. As I got older, I didn't want to incite the anger or get the "guilt trip" put on me for "being able to do things she wasn't able to do," especially "after all (she) had done for me." I just didn't want to hear that anymore. So I didn't ask permission to go out, even to the point of turning down some work reward trips! Foolish, in retrospect; but the alternative made me physically ill to fight the battle for permission to participate. So, I chose not to go.

There didn't seem to be a way of escape so, like the elephant, I just gave up and stayed "chained" to home.

This wasn't adult behavior, but I didn't know how to change my responses. Since I couldn't control my home life, I threw myself into my career. Perfectionism became a driver, along with a workaholic approach, to hopefully gain some approval - maybe even my own!

Some Uplifting Events ...

I was raised in church all my life it seems. We attended Baptist churches and believed in its disciplined teachings, including a strong belief in the 10 Commandments. I was often reminded of the one about "honoring thy father and thy mother." Any disrespect, such as talking back to father or my stepmother, would result in a reminder of that particular Commandment to enforce proper behaviors. This Commandment would strongly influence several of my life decisions, such as never leaving home and not marrying someone they didn't approve of.

I accepted Christ as my personal Savior at a Christian Summer camp when I was 9 years old. The speaker told us about the consequences of dying without knowing Christ as our personal Savior; he described Hell as a terrible place, on fire all the time and very lonely for all eternity. At the end of the message, he had us close our eyes and bow our heads; then, asked if anyone was afraid of going to Hell. Boy, did my hand shoot up fast! But then he wanted anyone who raised their hand to come forward. That was too scary for me, so I just sat there. But my camp counselor, Lil from Minneapolis, had peeked and saw me raise my hand! So, she spoke with me afterwards about God's love saving me from Hell, about accepting Christ as my Savior, and about God's gift of Eternal Life. It all sounded too good to pass up. So, I prayed for Christ to come into my heart and became a Christian! I was instantly healed, by the way, from a very bad sore throat I had since camp started that week! What a neat side benefit!

I was actually afraid to tell my stepmother and father that I made this decision without asking their permission. But accepting the Gospel message is a personal decision; so, I'm very grateful God convicted me to be independent and make that decision by myself. It was one I have never regretted. A lot can be taken from me in life, but I will never lose the joy of my salvation.

I tried to contact Lil, the camp counselor, in my adult years, but was unsuccessful; so, when I get to Heaven, I want to thank her for peeking that day and talking with me about this important decision in my life!

Surprisingly, my stepmother and father were actually happy for my decision!

It was a blessing to have excellent church youth group sponsors during my growing up years. My wish was to belong to their families. Mine just didn't seem normal or loving like theirs. The sponsors' love and devotion kept me close to God and active in church through the on-going struggles of my youth.

I don't know if I really changed outwardly that much because of my decision to follow Christ, but the frequency of the abuse seemed to ease around this age. My stepmother's total dominance over my life and my fear of her were still there. But some things had changed around my 9th year:

> *First*, my half-brother was born, which seemed to be a delight for my step-Mother … to have her own child. I remember that one of my daily chores was to fold my brother's cloth diapers. I was threatened, of course, with not being able to even hold my baby brother if I wasn't a good girl. Caring for him may have kept her busy and not so focused on my behavior issues.

> *Second*, my stepmother adopted me. I was to learn later that one of her adoption stipulations was that any contact with my birth mother or her relatives was to cease. Since I had been told my birth mother didn't want or love me, this didn't seem like such a big deal to me. I was told that my birth mother made no contact, nor contest, about the adoption. So, at this point, I didn't want anything to do with my birth mother either. If she didn't want me, I didn't want her.

I do remember going before the adoption judge and his asking me if I wanted my stepmother to adopt me. Out of fear of punishment and abandonment again, as I was led to believe my birth mother had done, I said "Yes," and the adoption wasm finalized.

I was not privy to read the adoption papers at this time, probably too young to understand them anyway. When I did obtain a copy of them, at 49 years old, from my stepmother's safe deposit box, those adoption papers held clues to assist with the major life changes that lay ahead for me.

Back to That First Counseling Session ...

Based on this background of my life to date, my response to the Counselor's question in that first counseling session will be easier to understand.

I clearly recall Beverly gently suggesting in that session, "I think it's time you found your birth mother."

To that I responded, "Why would I do that when she didn't want me or love me my whole life?"

Beverly inquired, "How do you know that?"

"My father told me," was my quick reply.

"How do you know he didn't lie about that?" Beverly asked.

I was totally silent. No one had ever mentioned that as a possibility. My father certainly must have heard me say many times, "How could a mother not love her child?!" So, certainly he couldn't have lied to me about my birth mother not wanting me, could he?? Had father never heard my stepmother's frequent accusation that "my mother didn't want or love me and that's why she left you," and not correct that thought if it wasn't true?? Surely father wouldn't have been that cruel, would he? All these thoughts quickly went through my mind and I dismissed the idea during that first session. Beverly knew there were many things for me to work on from what I had briefly shared already, so she didn't pursue this topic further at that time.

She proceeded to take notes as our conversation continued that first visit. She showed me some pain management techniques for better handling headache pain and recommended certain diet changes that might make a difference. Then she said that we needed to schedule some subsequent weekly sessions. It seems what I thought was to be just one visit, for answers about getting rid of my headaches, was just the beginning!

Beverly had learned some things in our initial meeting indicating there was far more to my migraines than just the airplane "bump on my head." More sessions were needed to unravel all of the mysteries. She wisely did not attempt to handle them all in the first visit.

I set some "boundaries" for these subsequent sessions:

They needed to be scheduled during an "extended lunch hour." I couldn't let it be known that I was in counseling, to avoid the stigma I thought was associated with it.

Anything that was determined to be an issue to be addressed needed to stop short of causing my stepmother any pain. In retrospect, that seems ludicrous considering the amount of pain she caused me! However, at this point, I was determined that, "she had done the best she could for me" and continued to excuse her "motherhood methods" due to her having an unhappy childhood, a difficult life, and then taking on someone else's child to raise. Often my stepmother had reminded me that I should be obliged to her for raising someone else's child, especially since I wasn't wanted or loved by my birth mother. Fortunately, my new Counselor was not accepting of these excuses; she knew many of these "fallacies" had to be undone … but not all in this one session.

Therapy to the Rescue …

At that point, Beverly knew the depth of my pain and said very sincerely, "Jan, I'm sorry I can't give you back your childhood. But I can help you move forward." And that's just what she did.

When Beverly realized the past abuse was a primary underlying cause of my issues, she worked with a psychiatrist who had been assigned to my case. I remember the doctor explaining to me that part of my brain had been hurt by the physical and verbal abuse, and that some medication would aid the physical healing process while going through the therapy sessions. I can't begin to do justice to the doctor's explanation, but it made sense. From a laymen's viewpoint it went something like: when one is abused, as I was, the brain starts shutting down the way it processes the actions to protect the person from the pain being inflicted. I recall he illustrated the process of "synapses misfiring," adding that the medications would heal the brain and allow the synapses to begin firing properly again. Sounded logical to me. The solutions Beverly and the doctor utilized did eventually yield good results, but only because they were coupled with her counseling and me doing my "homework" assignments!

Counseling is an interesting "taskmaster." While I first had reservations about going to any appointment or sharing anything about myself, I quickly learned that this was help being offered to me, and I should make the most of each appointment and the work required in between. God had arranged for it, at the right price, so I needed to get with the program!

I found myself living for those therapy appointments. I could hardly wait to discuss topics with Beverly because there was no one else who understood me or cared about me like she did as my Counselor. She believed I could get better and stronger, and encouraged me in those directions. She was the unbiased advocate for Janet Tombow! She was "in my corner" and that felt very good for a change. Helping me was a priority with Beverly, and it finally became a priority for me too.

I would race to an appointment on my lunch hour; bare my heart's concerns with Beverly; get my next therapy assignments; then race back to work and its hectic demands. I had to compartmentalize what I learned about myself at an appointment; compartmentalize assignments to be worked later, so I could concentrate immediately on work assignments; and compartmentalize working on the solutions until I had some space to allow my emotions to flow and then document them in my journals.

That night, when I was alone and very tired just before bedtime, I could finally start working on those assignments. This timeframe was when my stepmother would be in bed and no questions would be asked. She knew I was seeing a counselor for headache pain, but not for the root causes being discussed in detail relating to my relationship with her.

Little by little each assignment would help me work through the pain, and through my misconceptions or misguided thinking. Each would help me gain some healthy understanding needed. Through tears, prayers, self-analysis, and journaling, healing would take place. When the pain got particularly gut-wrenching, about half way through the counseling process, I asked God, "Why now in mid-life am I having to deal with all of these topics that hurt so much?" Later that night, He woke me up with the answer, "You weren't ready to handle this until now and I won't let you go through it alone!" That gave me great comfort and more strength for the journey to healing.

I would gradually move from idealism to reality; would release pent up anger, and change some co-dependent tendencies or better recognize when I was falling into that trap again. I would start to forgive some hurts, some people that were no longer in my life, and some things that couldn't be changed ever again in this lifetime.

I'm a very task-oriented person; love TO DO lists, and love even more TO DO lists with tasks marked as DONE! As I left one appointment, I would have a brief TO DO list of assignments. During the week, I would mark each assignment as DONE … or skip it if I didn't understand it or didn't want to work it.

As I would get ready for the next therapy appointment, I would consider what I had learned from last week's assignments, what I didn't get done or maybe some assignments I didn't want to do, along with explanations of why not. Then, I'd detail any new concerns or fears to be discussed at the appointment. That way I could make the most of each precious appointment, the short time Beverly and I would have together for me to keep getting well. The hour with her went so fast … but each time, I was one more hour closer to getting healed!

This counseling process continued for about 15 months, including a few months of group therapy sessions. Sometimes hearing the problems of others helps you with your own pain and vice versa. You can learn from each other.

The knowledge and insight gained helped me respond more properly to life. My journals indicate I had very few headaches now, that I had faced the abuse and forgiven what I could, that I was better overall. I had the tools now for a better life; I just needed to utilize them. For many months afterwards, I would continue to journal, as Beverly had recommended, whenever my thoughts would overwhelm and needed sorting out, or when something needed to be expressed and I didn't have anyone with whom I could safely do so.

I found the Counseling process extremely beneficial and do my best to recommend professional counseling to others, when I see their life situations becoming too overwhelming for them.

Things Can Get Worse …
About 1983, my father announced he had a two-week business trip that was taking him to Texas. He traveled some for work, so we hadn't thought anything of it when he was gone a few days on several occasions during the preceding few months. However, we were in the process of buying the house next door as a "family" rental property, when this Texas trip arose. When a question needed his input about the rental property, my stepmother contacted father's office to request he call her at his convenience; but the office informed her that father was on vacation, not on a business trip. What a total surprise! Father was calling home each night like he was on the road for business. So,

when he called that night, my stepmother questioned what he was doing on vacation, rather than on a business trip. That's how she learned about "the other woman" in his life.

It was a tough blow to both of us, certainly most devastating for her, but very disappointing for me having father do this when he had accused my birth mother of doing this to him. I couldn't understand how he could be doing this.

When he returned from Texas, naturally he and my stepmother talked about the marital issues, but it was a short conversation as he had his mind made up. He didn't care who he hurt; he felt justified in leaving her.

Before he left the house, I confronted him with my question, "How could you do this to Mom (my stepmother) when Norma (my birth mother) did that to you?" Father never answered me; he just left the house.

When I started counseling with Beverly in early 1992, I explained that some of my anger was from my father having left my stepmother for another woman, which left me to care for my abuser. I had my stepmother in my sphere of responsibility. She had no means of support since father had died several years previously. So, additional expenses fell to me to provide for.

All my stepmother would focus on was what she lost, not what she had. She always blamed the other woman, never father or herself for his leaving. But, due to my reluctance to confront the subject, I just let her continue on her self-pitying path and I continued my workaholic alternative.

Work was my escape, an "almost-acceptable" one from my stepmother's perspective. At times, she understood I had to provide for both of us now. At other times, she would call me numerous times a day at work to tell me unimportant things, like the mailman was late, and proceed to get angry when she'd find me in meetings unable to take her calls. She got angry if I had to work late, even if I called to let her know. She just didn't respect that I had a job to do. I was fortunate that work was patient with my home situation.

She never worked after she married my father; she had been totally dependent on him, she didn't even drive. As soon as he left her, I paid for her to take driving lessons, explaining I couldn't take time from work for shopping trips or outings she might want to make.

She didn't cultivate her own friends to do things with. Whenever acquaintances would ask her, she'd decline their invitations. She just wanted to go places with me, or make me feel guilty if I tried to do things on my own. My co-dependency allowed it. (That is my inability to handle feelings and behaviors in a direct, logical manner; it causes faulty communications, perfectionism, and inadequate boundary setting.)

My stepmother's despondency worsened.

A Breakthrough ...

At one point of frustration, I got courageous enough and told my stepmother she was, "a sick lady who needed to get help, or should get out of the house and do something" with her life.

She angrily responded that I was, "just like (my) father!"

I argued back, "Don't you ever compare me to him!" and informed her I was, "leaving for good!" I went to my room trying to figure out how to make good on my threat!

She followed me into the bedroom and raised her hand to strike me. I grabbed her wrist and in a very firm voice said, "Don't you EVER hit me again!" I could tell by the shocked look on her face that she believed me.

Finally, a breakthrough for me! I was 47 years old.

A Snowstorm Confrontation ...

It took many counseling sessions to unearth all the angry feelings, and deal with the consequences of that anger and my co-dependency. The anger just got stuffed, year after year, day after day, into the "garbage bags" of my mind; they never got emptied. The anger manifested itself in my migraines. However, the problem had to be dealt with at some point. God knew that ... and how to get that accomplished!

My stepmother and I were traveling back from visiting my half-brother and family in Nevada. We left early when we saw a storm closing in on Donner Pass Summit and I needed to be back at work timely the next day. As we approached the summit, the snow started, turning quickly into a blinding snowstorm! The side road markers weren't even visible, so we aimed for the middle of the road. Traffic slowed to a crawl. Safety did not seem a sure thing!

It actually took us 12 hours to go 20 miles. Those proved to be the longest 20 miles of my life! Trapped in the car with my stepmother who was increasingly unhappy with the changes in me as a result of the counseling help I was getting. She didn't like my attitude and the independence I seemed to be displaying.

So, I was forced to explain several things I wasn't happy with. (God was probably laughing at how He made this happen … finally!) I told her the counseling had made me understand the way I was living was abnormal and that things were going to have to change. Beverly had been trying to get me to have this type of conversation or confrontation for several months; but I kept saying I couldn't do it, I couldn't hurt my stepmother in my counseling process. God obviously thought it was time!

Since I was already "in the dog house" with my stepmother, this "captive audience" situation enabled me to ask some questions I had about my adoption process. I asked, "Did Norma, (my birth mother), ever respond to the adoption solicitation from the court?"

She said, "Oh yes, but we sent it back."

Although shocked, I pursued further, "Did Norma ever try to contact me before the adoption?"

Again, she nonchalantly said, "Oh yah! We received several letters but didn't respond to them."

I asked, "Do you still have those letters? I'd like to see them."

She said, "No, we tore them up, along with all the pictures of the past." Stated with no remorse, nor regrets, on her part. No acknowledgement that I had been lied to all these years. Those letters might have contained some important information or even comfort for me; but now I learned they were destroyed. I only had three pictures of me as a child; now I learned that's all I would ever have.

Once again, Beverly (my Counselor) had been right! There was more to the story than I had been given. I filed away this information to use at a later date. I couldn't handle anymore on this trip. I needed time and space to absorb what I learned and the consequences of it. Truthfully, I couldn't wait to get back to tell Beverly what I'd learned.

Things improved after this confrontation with my stepmother. She definitely didn't like the "new me," but I finally had the courage to tell her a few things I didn't like either! Counseling was paying off!!

More Bad News …

My suppressed anger was at its prime! God knew all about it.

During the year my migraines worsened, my stepmother's birthmark turned cancerous.

She would never go to the doctor like she was supposed to … to the point the doctor was yelling at me that he could help her if I'd get her in to see him sooner!

Little did I know at that time that she had told the doctor I wouldn't bring her to see him because of my work schedule. The truth was she was too afraid of any doctor to book an appointment and tell me when she needed to go. When I did take the initiative to book an appointment for her, an argument ensued in which I was informed that it was her life, not mine, and she would make an appointment only if she wanted to. This frustrated me because I knew her type of cancer could be cured by timely excising the diseased tissue, while other people had diseases that couldn't be cured! More anger for me - and more topics for counseling!

Over the next few years, my stepmother had five surgeries to excise Melanomas, but they kept returning and getting worse due to her delays in treatment. Her body wouldn't allow any more radiation therapy. The oncologist recommended her for an experimental drug treatment trial, but it failed after the first treatment.

At the age of 69, my stepmother died at home as she desired, with the help of Hospice care. With her bed surrounded by friends, we shared Scriptures and told stories, with Christian music playing in the background. My brother had been with us just a day prior. When her condition worsened suddenly, I called him to return. He was in route from Nevada. The exact minute his flight touched down at the airport, like she knew he arrived safely, my stepmother breathed her last breath. I believe that was a scene she didn't want him to have to endure. He and his family joined me for the funeral services.

I didn't have regrets as I did all I could for her as long as I could. It was good that God delivered her from her pain and deep depression. She never got over losing father.

Through therapy, I had learned to cope with her behavior. I tried to forgive the past and move on. I had recognized she was responsible for her life decisions, and I was responsible for mine.

All of a sudden, at 49, I was free from the responsibilities of taking care of someone. It was time for me to move on and live my life. My first thought was that I wanted to go on a trip, and could do so without having to ask permission or feel guilty! But it would be a while before I was truly able to move on.

When you watch a person take their last breath, it is a tough human experience. No matter how you feel about a person, when they die, it is a shock. It might be a relief in some ways, but there is a grieving process that occurs. You think you don't need to feel that grief, that you can handle the loss logically because you can't change it. But I couldn't handle this loss without help.

Time Alone to Learn More …

For the first time in life I was alone, a condition some probably would long for, and I probably should have welcomed. But God hadn't dealt with my anger yet. So, I wasn't content and He had more preparation in mind for me.

At a management weekend getaway, a colleague expressed sympathy about my recent loss. She added that it took her, "two years to get over the loss of (her) mother."

As I said, "Thank you." I quickly thought, "she already cost me lots of happy years of living so there's no way I'm going to mourn for two more years!" I determined to snap out of any depression and get on with my new life. Easier said than done.

For a few months, I thought I was doing pretty well, except for the uncontrollable need to clean all the time. Then, I responded unreasonably and angrily toward my neighbor who interrupted my cleaning by wanting to bring me a book to read. Feeling sad for me, she had just wanted to give me an empathetic hug. Instead of accepting it, I flew into a hurtful tirade! I was angry that she had treated my stepmother as a valued friend, rather than recognizing her for the dominating role she had played in my life. Her style was similar to my stepmother's of telling me what to do; she had brought over a book on grief telling me I needed to read it. After that comment and then trying to hug me, I over-reacted in anger. I asked her not to hug me, but she proceeded to try again. I backed away and told her I had enough to do without reading a book on handling grief, and that I had asked her to not hug me, but she kept insisting on doing so. This "co-dependent" was trying to set some boundaries, but not doing a very good job of it. At that point she left, naturally hurt by what I said and how I said it.

I was stunned by my reaction, and knew I better head back to Beverly for some counseling on handling my grief and, more specifically, my anger!

Value of Grief Counseling ...

I hadn't seen Beverly in about 3 years. Yet, at the first grief counseling appointment in late 1996, she didn't forget to tackle the subject again about me finding my birth mother.

To her suggestion, I said, "Why would I want to find another mother when I just buried one?"

Receiving that pointed response, she must have realized I truly did need some grief counseling!

We proceeded to examine and resolve a few key issues:

1. Did I do all I could for my stepmother?   "Yes."
2. Was I "saint-izing" my stepmother?   "Yes."

Beverly responded, "Well, stop it! Stop being a victim. Don't you remember all the things she did to you? She wasn't a good stepmother to you!"

"But she did the best she could," I defended.

Finally, Beverly challenged me with the truth, "Face it, Jan. What would a child of yours ever do that would cause you to treat your child the way your stepmother treated you?"

In tears, I responded, "I would NEVER treat a child that way!"

Healing began over the next several weeks. Anger was subsiding. I dealt with forgiveness needed toward my father and my stepmother, and worked on reducing my co-dependent tendencies. Beverly taught me that if you have more tears still to cry, you must cry them. She shared with me that you can love forever, but you don't have to grieve forever. She urged me to express all of my feelings and complete multiple other assignments to work through the grieving process.

My resolve was starting to soften when Beverly would continue to encourage me about finding my birth mother.

Another Little Push from God ...

It was the 1996 Christmas season. While cleaning the house, I played a Bill & Gloria Gaither Christmas video, "Joy to the World," on the TV in the background. I was singing along with their songs, as I often did.

When taking a break in the living room, a lady was speaking; her name was Lee Ezell. Basically, her story was that she was very glad she didn't abort her daughter, who was the result of a rape. She had given her up for adoption at birth. After several years, her daughter had contacted her most unexpectedly and reunited with her. Now she and her daughter were good friends. Lee introduced her daughter on the video. Both looked very happy and knew God had a plan for their lives … apart first … and now together.

It somewhat got my attention the first time that I saw this section of the video. As I continued during that week to replay the holiday video, do you know that every time I took a break, guess whose story was being told??!

After the third time I saw that story, I acknowledged, "Okay, God! I got the message! I know what you want me to do. Please give me the courage and show me how to do it."

Chapter 2

AN INTENSE SEARCH

"Who art thou that judgest another?"
James 4:12

Now that I had direction from God ... and from Beverly ... I knew I needed to get started on searching for my birth mother. There is no way I knew what a roller coaster ride this would be. Besides, I was clueless about how to get started!

The Lord made me very miserable on January 8, 1997, according to my journal entries. I wasn't happy; I couldn't concentrate at work; I couldn't forget that I needed to start looking for my birth mother, but was confused about where to start. After the holiday break, this misery was apparently to get me back on the recovery course and book another counseling appointment. Wouldn't you know, I was able to book an appointment for that very day!

Counseling Helps Again ...

At that session, Beverly spotted my reluctance to begin the search and took charge. She asked, "How do you think you can find your birth mother?"

"Well, I thought about signing up with 1-800-U.S. SEARCH," I responded.

Their frequent TV ads had intrigued me. After enrolling as a member of 1-800-U.S. SEARCH, and paying the up-front membership fee, the service is supposed to provide a list of possible matches and their phone numbers based on names and general vicinities you request of them. The requested information is returned to the member via U.S. Mail. Then, the member is free to pursue the contacts as they choose.

"Good idea!" she excitedly agreed.

I said, "Okay, I'll do it tomorrow."

"Oh no! Let's do it now!" she said. Do you think she knew I was trying to procrastinate?

Quickly, I stalled, "But I am not a member yet and I don't know what I will do with any contacts they do provide."

Beverly questioned further, "What do you mean you don't know what you'll do with any contacts they provide?"

"What if I called someone, and asked if she was my mother, and she hadn't told her family that she even had a child 50 years ago? That might hurt someone in their family," I countered.

Beverly quickly gave me her verdict, "What do you care? If she didn't tell her family, that's not YOUR problem!" This is a great example of the value of a counselor who has YOUR best interests, as her patient, in mind at all times! Remember, she was in my corner and committed to help me get well. I was letting this "What if" cause me anxiety that I needed to eliminate!

She then picked up the phone to "practice" a call I would make. She demonstrated how I would introduce myself and what I would ask of the answering party. She told me I needed to write out what I wanted to say to my birth mother if I connected. I left the session with the assignments of enrolling in 1-800-U.S. SEARCH and figuring out what I would say to my birth mother if I did make a call and found her.

I left the session understanding my assignments, but had not conquered the fear of making those calls. Remember, I had been raised on fear. So, this was looking like another chapter of that to me. It was the "unknown" that was scaring me. I wanted to be obedient, but the other part of me was terrified. The "What ifs" were abounding:

"What if I find her and have to face why she didn't want me??"

"What if she truly didn't love me??"

"What if she rejects me again? Can I handle it?"

And the list went on … with no one to answer these for me at this point!

A BIG Push from God this Time …

That night, on January 9, 1997, just to be sure I got HIS message … God gave me a literal wake up call at 3AM! I was washing my hands after a usual bathroom break, so I was pretty well awake. I looked in the mirror and heard the Lord say:

"Don't focus on the past, at what you've given up,
but look to the future at what you've been given."

WOW! That was so profound! There's no way I could have thought of that. The depth of its meaning was certainly nothing I think about at 3AM any night!

I quickly wrote down what God told me, so I wouldn't forget it. I would quote this numerous times in the months to come and even asked my friend, Pat, to memorialize it for me in a plaque which she framed for me. A beautifully framed memory, so I would NEVER forget this word from the Lord.

Launching the Search …

On January 9, 1997, I launched the search for "Norma Banks (maiden name)" or "Norma Tombow (married name)," of "Cleveland, Ohio," by giving those three pieces of information to 1-800-U.S. SEARCH … and waited for their response.

I had heard these searches for lost loved ones take years, or even decades, to get results. I wondered how long it would take me.

My fears weren't totally gone, and new ones surfaced daily. Now the "What ifs" included:

"What if friends, who knew my stepmother and family objected to my searching for my birth mother?"

"What if members of my own family objected?"

I knew I had to tackle these new fears at some point … but for now I had some tangible things to deal with, like my demanding job, nationwide travel required for the job, and my sick Chow puppy, Cricket, who was only six months old and had just been diagnosed with hip dysplasia. I was facing the prospect of having to put down this "little love" in my life or subject her to some serious surgery. These all were tangible challenges I was facing.

Now I had the intangible challenges too: the search for my birth mother and what to do if I found her. I had the direction to look for her, but I'm not sure I really had any hope of finding her. If I did connect with her, I had no clue what to ask to see if it was her; and if it was her, what would I say then??

Accessing Legal Papers ...

On January 12, I finally read my adoption papers thoroughly for the first time in my life - at 49 years old. They were in my stepmother's safe deposit box. I had never read them in great detail, only briefly looking at them previously, for they represented so many negatives in my life.

Now I needed to access them to learn any new facts that might expand the search criteria to give to 1-800-U.S. SEARCH. The adoption papers contained my birth mother's full maiden name, Norma Ellen Banks, and her birthplace, Cleveland, Ohio; but they also inferred that she may have married William Wallace, and may have lived in St. Louis or Detroit. Those facts could expand the search; but I decided to wait to see what 1-800 U.S. SEARCH came up with from the initial two pieces of information I provided.

I also accessed my birth certificate in the same safe deposit box, and was reminded of another negative from my past: my father and stepmother had my birth certificate altered. In "the old days," one was able to pay to have certain details altered on a birth certificate, and they had done that. My stepmother's information was now listed as the "name" and "birth date" of the birth mother. So, the birth certificate really didn't provide anything else I could use for the search. It only angered me again.

Meanwhile, work was going better. I was planning some business trips and planning a Greek Cruise vacation in May. Living alone was getting to be more comfortable. I appeared more content, believing I was doing what God wanted me to do.

That was until the first listing arrived from 1-800-U.S. SEARCH.

Working with the First Listing ...

There were three "Norma Banks" and no "Norma Tombow" on that first listing.

When the listing arrived on January 18, my journal indicates I went through several emotions:

Felt anxious ...

Was this search a betrayal of my father and stepmother?

Was I feeling guilty?

I certainly was frightened about the next step.

One concern was, "What am I getting myself into?"

How should the conversation go if I make the calls?

Felt angry ...

I'd been lied to all those years by my father and stepmother.

I needed to pursue the truth.

Felt afraid ...

Would I be in for more hurt in the search?

Did I want to get close to another mother after just watching one die?

If she wants to meet me, I'm not sure what I'll say.

Where do I get the courage to make the calls?

Need to get organized ...

Plan out the conversation for the cold calls to those on the 1-800-U.S. SEARCH listing.

Plan the conversation I would have with my birth mother when I connected.

Check on divorce papers, if I could locate them, for any other details to aid in the search.

Determine if forgiveness is needed and for whom. Did I need to forgive my birth mother for abandoning me? Was forgiveness needed for my abusive stepmother too? Did I also need to forgive father?

Cold Calling Experiences ...

On January 19, I made a list of the questions to ask in making cold calls. Then, took a chance and tried them.

During the first call to a "Norma Banks" shown on the 1-800-U.S. SEARCH listing, I inquired, "Is Norma Banks there?"

To that question, I was angrily informed, "She died 7 years ago!" and the lady hung up on me!

I panicked!

My first thought was "Oh no! I waited too long to make the call!" Now what was I going to do? Hadn't God told me to find her?! Had I failed?

It was a time for calm thinking to prevail. I didn't have a chance to explain to the first party why I was calling and try to keep her calm enough to answer a few other probing questions. Maybe THAT Norma Banks wasn't THE Norma Banks I was looking for. There were a few other Norma Banks' on the 1-800-U.S. SEARCH listing. Maybe another of the contacts would be the right one, if the first one was not my birth mother.

I didn't want to lose hope, but I did suddenly realize that I needed to face the possibility that my birth mother was dead. Could I handle that news?

During my callback to the first party, I asked a few more questions, "Was she married to my father, Edward Tombow?" I went on to explain they would have married in the early 1940's. Her answers were "No" to both questions, revealing that this Norma Banks was NOT my birth mother.

Whew! One down, two to go … on the listing.

The second call wasn't much better than the first! When I made the inquiry, I was informed that the second Norma Banks, "had Alzheimer's." So, the answering party offered to, "help me," as she was her daughter.

"Oh boy," I thought fearfully, "if this is the right Norma Banks, I would be speaking with my sister, and this could be a shock to her!" But I pressed on, asking if Edward Tombow could have been the lady's husband and stating they would have married in the early 1940's. Again, I was advised, "No," and learned this was not the right Norma Banks.

This response, however, also gave me a moment to consider, "What if I found out my birth mother had some serious illness, like Alzheimer's?" I really had given no thought to the possibilities of finding out she was dead or ill! Was I ready to face these kinds of issues??

There was a possibility I might not like what I discovered. But God had told me I must do the search, so I pressed on, with more realistic thinking in each call I made. My favorite verse, II Timothy 1:7, took on a whole new meaning at this stage of the search:

> **"For God hath not given us the spirit of fear, but of power, and of love, and of a sound mind."**

I had to keep this in perspective … and this verse became dearer with each call.

The other call I made from the 1-800-U.S. SEARCH listing was also a dead end.

Other Resources Accessed ...

I then called "Information" for lists of possible Norma Banks', Norma Tombow's, Norma Wallace's, or William Wallace's located in St. Louis, but there were several and "Information" doesn't like to give you more than one number or two at a time. So, I also contacted my employer's St. Louis regional office to ask if someone could look in the local telephone directory and copy for me any directory listings of the above names. They agreed to try and would mail them to me.

Meanwhile, I called some old friends and began to explain about my need to search for my birth mother. Surprisingly, they were all very supportive.

On the other hand, I still hadn't called my half-brother to explain my need to search for my birth mother. It was his birth mother who had recently died and, just after the funeral, I explained about my adopted relationship to my stepmother and that he was my half-brother. It was the choice of my stepmother and father to NOT tell my half-brother about my adoption by his birth mother. He grew up believing I was his sister by birth. I suspected that he might have questions as we went through the legal papers after she died. I felt it was time for total honesty, so we discussed the situation shortly after the funeral. I explained that I still loved him just as much as I did growing up; my love wasn't changed just because I was his half-sister.

Still, it was a big shock for him to absorb. From his perspective, he felt his father and mother had lied to him, and couldn't understand why they hadn't entrusted him with that knowledge at some point during his 41 years. For whatever reason, my father and stepmother chose to keep the adoption relationship a secret from certain friends and also from this important family member.

I could understand his distress and the need for time to accept the news. On the heels of that revelation, I wasn't sure how this search news for my birth mother would be taken. So, I decided I wasn't quite ready to deal with the fallout yet, if any were to occur. For now, I delayed any explanation to my family about this search getting underway.

The search was intensifying. Thoughts of finding her were on my mind constantly. I began to think of other resources that could be utilized.

More Facts to Digest ...

On January 20, I spoke with an old family friend named Joe. He used to work with my father in Ohio, just before father joined the Navy and after his discharge. I asked if Joe or his wife had any pictures of my father and my birth mother. He did and said he would send them to me.

Joe added some insight to the search "puzzle":

- Confirmation that my father and birth mother had married in 1944. From that fact, I felt better right away deducing that I wasn't illegitimate!
- Uncle Rich, my father's youngest brother, lived with my father and birth mother when growing up. Joe said my birth mother wouldn't permit Uncle Rich to live in the house, so a room was built over the garage. He provided me with Uncle Rich's telephone number from the Ohio directory.
- Father had worked two jobs to satisfy my birth mother's wants and expensive tastes.
- Father was skinny. So, when he heard that my birth mother ran off with a "big, fat, ugly guy," he didn't understand it.
- Joe claimed that there was "no better man with morals at that time" than my father.
- When I asked if my birth mother worked, Joe said she worked part time at an expensive department store.
- He said she attended work baseball games.

With some trepidation, I called my Uncle Rich, with whom I hadn't spoken in several decades. It seems that after the adoption all family contacts in Ohio ceased - not just with my birth mother and her family.

I spoke with Uncle Rich's daughter-in-law, Barb. I explained who I was and why I was trying to reach him. She told me he was out of town, which made my heart sink. Another delay, I thought. But she said she would give him the message.

I'm actually surprised Barb followed through, as emotional as I was on the call. I figured she probably thought I was a "nut case," as I sobbed through our conversation. Several times she had to ask me to repeat myself, I was so incoherent. I said I hadn't been drinking, was just emotional! She expressed understanding.

The emotions surprised me. Now that I thought I was getting one step closer to contacting my birth mother, I couldn't get my tears under control. These "rehearsal" conversations began to formulate what I wanted to discuss with my birth mother, when and if I really did find her. But each call increased my emotional response to the search.

My Talk with Uncle Rich ...

When my Uncle called back the next day (January 21), he expressed his delight in talking with me after all these years. He understood my desire to locate my birth mother; and, with that in mind, shared what he recalled as a young person who lived with my father and birth mother:

- He lived with them 2½ years, as a teenager, until marital problems developed between my father and birth mother. After living somewhere else one year, my Uncle returned to live with my father and birth mother again.
- He had to take me to the ballpark and look after me if he wanted to play ball, because he was the "sitter" while my father and birth mother worked.
- Father and William Wallace, identified as the man my birth mother ran off with, actually played on the same church softball team.
- He remembered that my birth mother did take care of me; remembered her curling my hair; and said she never tried to kill me. So, I learned I was cared for! Another BIG plus for me!!
- He said my birth mother was a sportswriter trainee at a local newspaper when he first met her. This was interesting to know as it might have accounted for my love of sports. It seemed like this would have been a tough occupation for a woman to succeed in back then. So, that meant to me that she had talent and ambition.
- When my birth mother left my father, he and I went to live with my birth mother's parents. But Uncle Rich didn't know why she had left. Uncle Rich remained living at father and my birth mother's old house.
- About a year later, father told Uncle Rich that someone was taking him to court for custody of me. The next thing Uncle Rich remembered was that father, my great grandparents, and I left Ohio for California. (My comment to Beverly, "Do you have to be right all the time?!" There obviously was more to the story than I was being told!)
- Uncle Rich said my maternal grandparents loved me a lot and confirmed we had lived with them for a year. They babysat for me while father went to work. But after father took us to California, my grandparents never saw me again.

It made sense to me that my grandparents, my birth mother's parents, must have loved me a lot, as they both left me inheritances several years later. I declined them, however, because I was principled or too stubborn. If my birth mother and her family didn't want me when I was growing up, they shouldn't try to "buy me" with this type of gift when one of them dies.

When my grandfather died, I specifically remember being at a Christian Singles Conference when I was paged to a telephone call. It was my father stating that my grandfather had died and left me an inheritance, and the attorney needed to be in touch to see that I received it. I replied, "I don't want it."

He asked, "Are you sure?"

I replied, "If they didn't want me when I was growing up, they shouldn't try to buy me now."

That was my father's opportunity to let me know they DID want me, or to change the story that I had grown up with; but he didn't say anything except that he would let the attorney know. Consequently, I turned down the inheritance. (Please keep this thought in mind, as I'll explain the further consequence of this decision in a later chapter of this book.)

More Clues About the Past ...

Uncle Rich added more details to aid my understanding:

- He met my stepmother in 1955. He recalled how firm she was with me, thinking she was pretty tough on just a 7 or 8 year old kid. He confirmed she made me practice accordion one hour daily.
- Several years later, Uncle Rich tried to see father when he and his daughter visited California; but apparently, my stepmother stonewalled that idea and told him father couldn't see him. At a reunion in Ohio, after father had left my stepmother, father said he never got the message that Rich was in town and wanted to see him.
- I shared with Uncle Rich about the abuse I endured. He questioned if I was sure it was true; I said, "Absolutely!" He commented that father may not have been strong enough to stand up to my stepmother and stop what was happening.

Based on all of this information provided by my Uncle, my stepmother had lied and so did father, by his silence! Apparently, I WAS loved and cared for by my birth mother. My journal notes say, "I'm not sure if I feel sad, angry, or disappointed at this point, but I am emotionally tired, just by what I have learned so far." I felt bad if my birth mother regretted what she did; I further regretted that I had disliked her so much all of these years. But I did resent that she abandoned me based on what I was told. I again felt betrayed for being beaten for lying as a child, only to realize how much lying I was a victim of!

Uncle Rich added:

- He thinks my birth mother is in Florida.
- He mentioned my birth mother's sister's name, saying she was a nice lady. I recognized the name, "Aunt Phyl," but didn't recall anything about her.
- He asked me to come see him soon. I said I would, but needed to get this search resolved first.

Calls to More Resources ...

Another friend provided the name of an organization for me to contact in Seattle, Washington. It was an adoption registry, for adopted persons to be listed hoping to be found in case a parent wanted to locate a child they had put up for adoption. I spoke with a nice man at that organization and registered to be listed as a candidate for contact, if my birth mother chose to look for me some day using this resource.

Based on the new information gathered, I again called 1-800-U.S. SEARCH and expanded the search criteria. Not only had my Uncle Rich provided some new facts, like my birth mother might be in Florida, rather than St. Louis or Detroit, but the adoption papers had given me the other possibility that she now had the last name of Wallace.

A different friend started planning my 50th birthday party! She called to ask me who I'd like to have invited to the party to celebrate my February 24 birthday. This was a nice break from all of the serious search activities!

What Do I Need to Do Now? ...

Over lunch on January 22, I made this listing to sort out what needed to be done next, based on what I'd learned:

- Ask Uncle Rich if he knows the whereabouts of Aunt Phyl, my birth mother's sister.
- Make contacts when another 1-800-U.S. SEARCH listing arrives.

- Meet with Beverly to see how to deal with the guilt I'm feeling doing this search so close to my stepmother's death. I'm especially having trouble handling the feedback from my stepmother's friends who thought highly of her, when I'm not feeling that, the more I'm learning. I know I need to stop being a victim after what my stepmother did to me and all her lies.
- Decide how to deal with the truth of what I'll learn.
- Contact other adoption agencies or registries, if 1-800-U.S. SEARCH yields no additional contacts.
- Pursue other telephone listings I'll be receiving and make those calls too.

How Do I Feel Now? ...

I prepared another list of thoughts and feelings that I needed to sort out:

- Glad to be on the trail to truth; glad there are some positives about my birth mother I'm already hearing.
- Feel a little nervous or anxious about what lies ahead.
- Still want to talk with my birth mother.
- Unsure how soon I'd want to see other relatives. They are like strangers to me, they have been off-limits for so long. Angry I lost many years of their acquaintances for wrong reasons. Suspicious, that stepmother lied about a lot of things, which led to strained relations.
- Feel disloyal to be seeking these answers so close to stepmother's death. But I'm angry at the way she treated me.
- Relieved that old friends are being supportive, when I was concerned they could have been unkind towards this search in process.
- Thankful for the prayers of my current friends; they are very supportive and interested in results; they feel it's like watching one of those TV shows about a reunion after 40+ years!
- Thankful for Beverly being available to me to assist with my uncertainties. She keeps encouraging me and probes as needed for my good.
- Thankful to God that He is so near in each step of this search; He is being gentle with me to give me "little bites" of this "big elephant" in my life.
- Sorry I've lost so many years; but need to keep looking at what I've been given, not what I've given up from the past.
- Sad about my birth mother having to live with her loss, if she truly regretted her decision; sad for my grandparents too that they never got

to see me again.

- Scared to meet my birth mother on the heels of the hurt of my stepmother's death. Unsure I want to have another mother in my life I could lose or have to take care of.

Other than this, I think I have things under control!!

More Contacts to Make ...

Just when I would get discouraged, someone came along to encourage me. They provided a listing of calls to be made; the name of another organization who could help; or a friend just said they were praying for me.

On January 23, Sally, my dear friend who has been a great encourager about this search from the start, copied more phone listings at the library. These lists were for "Norma Wallace" and "William Wallace" in the St. Louis area.

With Sally's latest listings in mind, I took a half day off work to make the calls to the East Coast; after work is really too late to make those calls. Several numbers were disconnected. No success with others contacted ... more dead ends. I was getting a little frustrated!

I finally am getting obsessed with God's direction to find my birth mother; it is constantly on my mind.

An Adoption Registry Match?? ...

I obtained a list of adoption information contacts from another friend. At a Nevada Registry the volunteer was most helpful, and I had to face another challenge. He potentially located my birth mother within his Registry's records based on the pieces of information I had compiled to date. The 1925 birth date fit, as did the full maiden name; and her place of birth was listed as Ohio. I needed to get a copy of a form to confirm Norma's mother's and father's names, to be sure it was her. This required me to complete two forms he was sending me.

The problem was this Norma Ellen Banks (my birth mother's maiden name) died in 1966 in San Bernardino, California. Can you believe it? Just 20 miles away from where I lived. So, I needed to obtain a copy of her death certificate, to be sure it was her.

The fact that this lady died in 1966 gave me a little comfort, because it took me 5 years to get the message from God to find her. So, it isn't like I just missed finding her. But I did miss finding her while operating under the lies I grew up believing. That makes me angry. I think I have some forgiving to do, I am so angry about being lied to so much.

On January 25, I received the death certificate. This confirmed the Norma Ellen Banks who died in San Bernardino was NOT my birth mother.

The roller coaster ride continues ... up and now down again!

Some Uplift from Discouragement ...

The wedding pictures arrived today from my old Ohio friend, Joe. I see my father, birth mother, and the wedding party at their wedding. She looked beautiful; he looked skinny but handsome in his Navy uniform. I see them with Joe and his wife at the wedding reception.

Will I ever see my birth mother again in this life, I wonder?

Meanwhile, my puppy was diagnosed as needing $2,500 to $5,000 in surgery to fix her hips. I'm not sure that is what should be done. I spoke with a friend who will help get a second opinion. This distresses me further, with all the other pressures of the search.

With this sad news, I lose some interest in making more calls.

Then, Sally rushes up to my door with more listings off the Internet. So, I proceeded to make 30 more calls to "Banks" or "Wallace" contacts. No luck yet.

I got the courage to call my half-brother and let him know what was going on. My sister-in-law took the call and told me my brother was working and asked, "What's going on?"

I told her about God telling me to find my birth mother and about how the search is going, or actually the frustration of it all at this point. My sister-in-law was very encouraging, telling me not to get discouraged; she assured me that if anyone can find her, I could.

She thought it was exciting and a great goal for me to work on. She said to let them know if there's anything they can do. I just asked her to let my brother know what I was doing and told her I'd call them with any progress reports.

On January 27, I left on a business trip.

News on my Cricket was good when I called home. She doesn't need the surgery; medicine can help her live comfortably. I am so relieved.

Now I can refocus on the search ... but must handle work priorities first!

The Search "Roller Coaster" Dips Again ...

After a good day at work, I made several calls from the hotel on January 29 to "Wallace" and "Banks" contacts from Sally's listings, but with no luck.

I returned from the business trip, but work remained a priority, and the search seemed to be going nowhere.

I received another listing from 1-800 U.S. SEARCH on February 5. At that point, I faced the fact I was afraid to start calling again. If I make these calls, one of them might be her, and that is still scary. So, I procrastinated again and didn't do any calls from home after work.

A few friends called on February 8 and gave me some encouragement about the search.

I met with Sally over lunch and discussed possible next steps for the search. We went to the library together and got contacts from newspapers in the Cleveland area.

Sally also located a Mormon Church who has genealogy search capability and records. However, they were not helpful with my search needs.

I finished the registrations for the AAC (American Adoption Congress, National Headquarters in Washington, D.C.) and the AAC Reunion Registry (in Nevada). There are more of these registry organizations listed in the Resource section of this book.

I also called a contact I had through work at the Social Security Administration (SSA). My contact gave me the address for sending a letter to someone you are trying to locate, and reviewed the procedures with me. A composed letter can be sent to SSA, along with payment of the fee required for researching where the letter should go, and for the cost of mailing it. With the letter to be forwarded, one must list all of the details known about the letter's addressee, to assist the SSA in locating that person. If the SSA can locate that party, the letter is forwarded. The recipient then has the option of contacting the originator or not.

This required me to compose a letter to my birth mother. But I wasn't sure what I wanted to say. After giving it some thought and prayer, this is what I chose to write to my birth mother:

2/8/97

Dear Norma,

I've been trying to locate Norma Ellen Banks (maiden name), who was married to Edward Charles Tombow in 1944, and to William Wallace in 1955 (approx), and who gave birth to me on 2/24/47.

> *(NOTE: These are the only facts I could supply to help SSA locate her in order to forward the letter. If you can provide the Social Security Number, the search is much easier; but I didn't know my birth mother's).*

If this describes you as my birth mother, I'm writing at this time for the following reason:

> All my life I was raised to believe that you left me because you didn't want me. I was told you never even cared enough to contact me, and I've carried bitterness and sadness in my heart wondering "How could a mother not want her child and just leave her child without ever looking back?"

> But about 4 years ago, through therapy and research, I learned that what I was led to believe all my life was not the total truth. You did try to contact me and the letters were destroyed (or returned).

> Recently I learned more about you and want very much to talk with you, to learn the truth about the situation, and to ask your forgiveness for the bitterness I've felt all my life, which has led to my never trying to contact you before this. The Lord has convicted me that "who am I to judge anyone for what they've done" and especially based on untruths?

> So, if you are willing to talk and want to contact me, please do so at: *(home and work contact information provided).* Feel free to call collect.

> If you don't wish to talk, or are unable to contact me, please know that I'm sorry that I've had the wrong story all these years that has kept us apart. I would not want any sadness or bitterness you may feel to keep you from knowing the God I love, Who forgives us of any wrong doing if we just ask.

> Love,
>
> Your daughter,
>
> Jan Tombow

I'll let you know what happened with this letter in a later chapter. But this exercise helped me know what I needed to say to my birth mother, if I was able to speak with her some day.

Another Gentle Confirmation from The Lord ...

I attended church on February 9, 1997 and the sermon must have been designed just for me! The sermon was based on **James 4:12** (which says: **"There is one lawgiver, who is able to save and to destroy. Who art thou that judgest another?"**).

In my Bible that day, I wrote at the end of the book of James, and still have these words inscribed from 2/9/97:

> "James 4:12 – why I must search for my birth mother; I've judged
> her all of my life and need to right this wrong; and maybe she wants
> to be forgiven – or at least needs to seek the Lord's forgiveness and
> bitterness or un-forgiveness could keep her from knowing the Lord."

Isn't it interesting that the day prior I wrote the SSA letter talking about this "judging" subject?! So, there was no doubt I was on the right track! But what is the next step??

A "Norma Wallace" Returns my Call ...

While doing some chores after church, the telephone rang. I answered, "Hello."

The voice on the telephone said, "Hello, this is Norma Wallace." At this point, I stopped what I was doing and my heart started racing. I thought I was speaking with her at last!

Whenever I made calls and left messages to the people who might have been my birth mother, I always asked them to feel free to call me "collect." That way, I could be sure the cost of calling back wouldn't prevent me from hearing from her. Sometimes I received returned calls, but interestingly no one ever called me back "collect." This call was not a "collect" call either, which could have given a little warning. Instead, I was caught off guard when she announced she was "Norma Wallace."

But she quickly added, "I'm sorry that I'm not your birth mother. I wish I was because I know this is important to you, but I'm not the right Norma Wallace. I wish you luck in finding your birth mother." Again, another roller coaster up and dropped!

But I thanked her for calling … and realized something else for the first time. In all the calls I had made from the call listings, I never understood how it would feel to get a "cold call" asking if the answering party was THE "Norma Wallace" who was my birth mother. It would be a shock to her. That gave me some additional sensitivity I needed in this journey.

This call ignited my desire again to find my birth mother. So, I was led to call back my Uncle Rich.

A Key Discovery …

When Uncle Rich answered my call, I said, "I am obsessed with finding Norma. Do you know anything else that might help me get in contact with her?"

Quickly he responded, "I found her sister, Phyllis, listed in the Cleveland telephone book. She still lives in the same house she did for all of her life. I called her and she wants to talk with you."

I never asked him why he didn't call me with this information sooner. I guess he didn't call, waiting to see if I truly wanted to find her. Or else sooner would have rushed the timing of my preparation. I needed to go through all of these steps to be ready for the contact with my birth mother.

"Does she know if Norma is alive?" I eagerly asked.

"Norma is alive and living in Florida," Uncle Rich answered and reiterated, "and your Aunt's eager to talk with you." So, he gave me her telephone number before I hung up.

I was still eager to make the connection to Norma, so I didn't hesitate to make the call to my "Aunt Phyl," as I remembered she was called. I didn't remember anything about what my Aunt looked like, how close our relationship had been, or when I had seen her last. But my first priority was to find out how to contact my birth mother, and this was finally the right connection I needed to be able to finally reach her.

When Aunt Phyl answered the call, she seemed very happy to hear from me. I explained who I was and that I "wanted to reach my mother, Norma Wallace."

She asked, "Why do you want to talk with her?"

For a moment I wanted to say that I'd prefer discussing that with my mother. But I was afraid to offend this direct link to finding my mother. So, I went through the logic of, "wanting to ask her forgiveness for judging her all my life and explain why I haven't been in touch before this."

She surprised me by saying, "I'll have to call her to see if she will talk with you, because there has been so much hurt over this, you know!"

I thought to myself, "You're darned right there has been hurt over this!" But instead of verbalizing that, I said, "Please see if she will talk with me," and gave her my telephone number.

It wasn't more than 15 minutes later and the telephone rang. I thought it would be my birth mother, so with some trepidation, I answered, "Hello?"

To my disappointment, it was Aunt Phyl again. She called me back with the update, "I spoke with Norma and she wants to talk with you." Now I was getting hopeful, but then she added, "but she wants you to call her because she's afraid you'll hang up on her if she calls you."

That didn't sound like a problem, so I said, "I will call her." Then, she gave me my birth mother's telephone number in Clearwater, Florida. (By the way, William Wallace in Clearwater, Florida was on one of the lists Sally had given me; I just hadn't reached that point in the call lists yet! I concluded that the contact was not supposed to be made via a "cold call.")

Aunt Phyl wanted to talk a few minutes more, while I was eager to make that next call! But I was polite, and took the time to converse with her briefly. Aunt Phyl told me a few interesting things that I didn't realize had occurred. She asked, "Do you remember playing with Rusty (her son and my cousin)?" But I didn't have that memory either.

Then, she mentioned she had letters from me, as she used to correspond with me when I was a little girl. Surprised, I questioned, "You have letters that I wrote??"

She added, "Yes, and from your stepmother too!"

I told her, "I don't remember writing those letters. But my stepmother used to write out the words for me when I was little, and I copied them into letters to people. So maybe that is what happened." This was another memory of which I had no recollection, nor did I want to dwell on it. When I copied those letters, I remember getting verbally and physically abused if I made any mistakes. Not a happy memory!

I didn't know I wrote letters or received any from relatives for all of those years I had been apart from my birth mother. I thought no one wanted anything to do with me. So, hearing about these letters was a big surprise.

She added, "I saved them. I hope you'll come to see me and I'll show them to you."

Now, my Aunt Phyl AND my Uncle Rich wanted me to come see them. But I could only focus on the goal of talking with my birth mother. So, I promised to visit in the future, but couldn't promise when. We ended the conversation at that point.

Contacting the "Right" Norma Wallace ...

Now I had the right phone number for the RIGHT Norma Wallace ... but my first thought was, "Okay, what do I do now?"

I know this seems like a foolish thought at this stage of the search, but I was very nervous all of a sudden. After the two years of therapy, hundreds of counseling assignments, five years of knowing I was supposed to contact my birth mother but resisting, and now after an intense 30 day search, I was just one phone call away from talking with her. But I'm thinking, "The time's finally come to make that call, but what if she rejects me again? What if she's angry with me?"

The "What ifs" were attacking me again! So, I went to the bathroom, I was so nervous! That seemed like a reasonable stall!

While there, God said, **"What do you mean, what should you do?? It's time to call her!"** God just wouldn't let it go, would He! After all, He had been arranging this moment in time for over 45 years! He doesn't give up. It's just that sometimes we're too stubborn to listen! So, I thought, "I had better obey!"

I grabbed a tablet and pen. I took a couple of deep breaths and picked up the telephone. It only rang a few times, and then I heard her say, "Hello."

"Hello. Is Norma Wallace there?" I inquired.

"Speaking," she replied.

Another deep breath and bravely I went on, "This is Janet Tombow and I think I'm your daughter." Now the moment had come. What would she say??

Gently, she said, "Hi Sweetheart, how are you?"

WOW! What a loving response. She didn't yell at me. She didn't hang up. She didn't say, "It's about time!" or "What took you so long?" That was pretty encouraging!

Now it was my turn to figure out what to say next. Tentatively I said, "Well ... I'm not sure; but I think I'm a little older than when you saw me last." Brilliant, right?!

She chuckled and said, "I think so!" She had last seen me at 5 years old, and now I was approaching 50.

It was my turn to speak again already, and I realized, even though I had rehearsed it several different ways, I didn't know what to say next! So, I said, "Even though I've called over 250 people across the country asking them if they were my mother, now that I've found you, I don't know what to say next."

Gently she offered, "Why don't you let me start?"

With that, she proceeded to explain much about the past that I didn't know. I was still thinking that she didn't want me or love me my whole life. So, I was listening with a doubtful and hostile heart. She wasn't hesitant about answering any of my questions and promised to be honest with me.

Learning About Our Separation ...

Then, a most shocking statement was made next, "When your father kidnapped you from me, I was never able to get you back!" Holy smokes! Kidnapped??! That was something even Beverly, my Counselor, hadn't suggested, and definitely wasn't part of any explanation I heard over the years. She added, "Whenever I'd go to a different state, we (her and her second husband) would hire an attorney to try to get you back. But the attorney would say, because you were in California, there was no hope of recovering you from your father."

She explained that she had been married to my father for seven years, and had been married to her current husband, Bill Wallace, for almost 40 years. She concluded she didn't think all of the problems of getting along with my father were hers, if she could stay married to her second husband for 40 years. She shared with me that there is a big difference between being "loved" and being "cherished," and her second husband definitely "cherished" her.

She said that she had believed God didn't intend for her to live the rest of her life in misery, if she and my father were not able to get along after seven years. Father had been a very controlling person, had a bad temper (which I had observed many times; he even used boxing gloves one time and punched a neighbor!) He was verbally abusive to her or gave her the silent treatment rather than working through problems (of which I had first-hand knowledge.) He had always put his family ahead of mother and me; he didn't consult my mother on our family's decisions; later, his brothers consistently came before my mother and me, based on a deathbed promise to his mother to take care of the family. My mother was treated like a slave for the family rather than a wife. There were several other incompatibilities that would take time to be unveiled, as our time of sharing went beyond this initial conversation.

I learned that her childhood had also been a very abusive one, like mine. Her mother would hit first and find out who was at fault later, with no apology if mother had not been at fault at all. Her mother was very controlling, as well as physically and verbally abusive. So, when father was treating her similarly after seven years of marriage, I had to respect that she decided she wasn't going to continue living in her marriage like she had grown up. I only wish I would have had that courage to leave the abusive life I grew up in.

So, when mother decided she had to do something besides staying married to my father and being miserable, she had gone to a local attorney. He told her to go to another city, after leaving me with someone who loved me and would care for me, which were her parents. At her lawyer's advice, she was to establish herself in a different location; he told her to get a job there, to prove she could take care of herself and me. Then, she should pick me up from her parents and start her new life in that new location.

Meanwhile, her mother had invited my father to move in with them, stating I was crying all the time. Besides that, her mother liked my father. I learned that while my father was in the Navy, her mother corresponded many times with my father, signing the letters as if written by my mother! That's how much my grandmother liked my father and how deceitful she was. When my father came home on leave and told my "mother-to-be" that she wasn't responding to him like her letters indicated, she questioned, "Letters?" He said, "Yes, all those letters you wrote to me while I was away." Here the letters weren't even from my mother; they were from HER mother! Talk about starting a relationship on a shaky foundation! But her mother apparently never gave up on liking my father!

At the time my mother was planning the divorce, my theory is that getting a divorce was not a popular or acceptable option. So, I believe the family was taking sides against my mother in favor of my father, which was how he ended up living with me at her parents' house.

Mother had done just what her attorney advised her to do. But, with father and me living at her parents, it could appear that mother had abandoned me. So, the custody battle was expected to be difficult to prove mother was a fit mother.

However, my father heard that it was time for mother to file for divorce and custody, and my mother was going to retrieve me from her parents. So, while my grandparents were at a bowling banquet one night, father cleared all of my things and his from the house; he picked up my great-grandparents; told Uncle Rich of the plan to leave due to the custody fight upcoming; and left town for California.

My mother's parents came home to an empty house and were totally surprised. They were shocked my father could be so heartless.

My mother was heartbroken and never saw me again. She said after I had been kidnapped she almost lost her mind. She was crushed that I had been taken from her. She lay on the bed crying, when a thought came to her, but she didn't know where it came from. Many years later she would hear those words again in church. What she heard that sad day were the first two verses of Psalm 121:

**"I will lift up mine eyes unto the hills.
From whence cometh my help?
My help cometh from the Lord, who
made heaven and earth."**

She was grieving. She was devastated and lonely for a very long time. In effect, her family had turned against her. She really had no friends with whom to share this loss, because she was living in a new city trying to make a new life. She tried to work, but it was hard to be in retail sales or banking and wear a smile on her face, when her heart was breaking on the inside.

It wasn't until several months afterwards that Bill, now her second husband but then just an acquaintance, showed up in the town in which mother lived. She knew him from the church softball games prior to the kidnapping. Apparently he had been married at that time, but was now separated. He came to town offering mother a friendship, and they began dating after being friends for several months.

After they married, she said she was only able to handle the loss by compartmentalizing it. She said, after awhile, it wasn't fair to her second husband to continue to openly grieve. She had to choose to go on living if there was no way to recover me.

However, in every state my mother and Bill moved to, they consulted with a new attorney to see what could be done to recover me. Consistently, they were told, "nothing could be done, California takes care of its own; and you can never afford to fight it." All attorneys were appalled at the advice given mother by her Ohio attorney. To this day, mother does not have a kind opinion about attorneys!

Even more appalling to the attorneys, however, was the fact that her mother and father took in my father and me. That made it appear like abandonment by my mother. One of the attorneys actually confronted mother's parents, asking why they did that. The attorney ended the meeting telling her parents they should be ashamed of what they did to their daughter.

So, it appears part of the fault was with mother's parents. But at this stage, I can't judge, I just must press on with this step in locating mother.

They actually didn't stop trying to recover me until she thought I didn't want her. (Remember the rejection of the inheritances? It had been conveyed to my mother that I didn't want anything to do with her. The part about me believing "she didn't want me" was never conveyed. There was a second side to the story, but neither of us heard the other side. Consequently, we were separated for 45 long years.) Rejecting the inheritances meant to her that I didn't want her. When she believed that, she had to give up hope of our reconciliation forever.

Special Insight into Mother's Loss …

Tearfully and still not believing that she truly wanted or loved me, I asked her if she "ever thought about me during all those years?"

She responded, "Oh Honey, your birthday and Mother's Day were the hardest days of the year for me, every year you were gone. Fortunately, Bill would be considerate on those days and encourage me to take the car, go down by the beach, have lunch out, and give me the space I needed to grieve by myself."

Just recently, a friend of mine helped me understand the depth of this loss for my mother. Every year for 45 years, she had to be reminded of my having been taken from her. She mourned every birthday, every holiday, especially every Mother's Day. Every time there was a baby shower, or an employee who had child issues, or got pregnant, she would be reminded of having lost me. My mother and Bill didn't tell their friends about me for all of those years; a secret that only they bore. Fortunately, Bill loved and cared enough for my mother to allow her the time and space needed on those days she couldn't handle the memories or when mourning would overtake her heart. He never told her "get on with it; she didn't want you; why don't you give it up?!" Instead, he was a compassionate listener and lover who cared more about her happiness than his own.

When a parent chooses to give up a child, it's generally for want of a better life for them. But mother didn't have a choice. She lost someone she loved and wanted, but could not get back. Later, she had to face the thought that I didn't want her. She had rejection to face, in addition to her never-ending grief.

It's hard for me to comprehend how she never lost her mind and chose to go on living. That took a very strong woman, with an extra strong love from and for her second husband, and an implicit trust in the Lord for strength and comfort.

When Aunt Phyl Made her Call ...

When Aunt Phyl first called mother, she told her to "sit down" because she had "some shocking news" for her. Aunt Phyl said I had called to ask if she knew how to be in touch with Norma because I wanted to speak with her. Mother said she'd have to call Phyl back because she had to think about it. Mother was so shocked that I finally had contacted her, she wasn't sure if she could handle a conversation with me. Apparently, she was as nervous in Florida as I was in California.

Mother told Bill that I had called Phyl and wanted to talk with Norma. Mother asked Bill what he thought she should do. Concerned only with what was best for mother, as was typical of Bill I would later learn, he responded with, "Do whatever you want, Honey. Do you want to talk with her?" Mother responded, "Yes," and called Phyl back asking that I contact her. She believed if I initiated the call I wasn't as likely to hang up on her to hurt her again. Mother feared rejection and hurt, as much as I did.

However, the conversation was much more positive than expected. It went well, that is, after I stopped being so angry and mistrustful. Hearing I had been kidnapped shifted my anger to the more deserving parties.

We exchanged some history about each other. I explained my anger about the abuse and being stuck with my stepmother after father left. She shared many things about her life with and after father.

I did tell mother that Aunt Phyl said she had letters from me and from my stepmother. Mother said, "Letters, what letters?" Apparently, mother had never been told that Aunt Phyl corresponded with my stepmother or me; she was never told the family knew how to be in touch with me, or where I was located. This was another obvious betrayal by her family, which hurt deeply. However, mother was afraid to ever challenge Phyl about the betrayal. Mother didn't want to be responsible for her older sister having a heart attack, if an argument started, as angry as mother was about that deception. So, mother chose to keep silent about those letters. I didn't bring them up again either. They had caused enough hurt.

Getting Acquainted Facts ...

Mother was in good health fortunately. During that first call, I had a sudden vision of the "bag lady on the corner" of a nearby Southern California neighborhood. What if she was like that lady? Could I handle that, if I found her wanting or needing help? Before I called, I gave no thought to that possibility. What I did have was clear direction from God to find her, so I could only trust this reunion was going to work.

Likewise, mother had no clue what my living situation was like. I could have been contacting them needing financial help, or worse, I could have been a person on drugs or alcohol! But she too trusted that my contact was sincere and was willing to talk with me without knowing many of the particulars about my life.

After working in Detroit, owning a business in St. Louis, and working hard for years in Florida in real estate and banking, mother and Bill decided to retire in Clearwater, Florida, in a nice condominium complex. The complex had many activities in which they could be involved, like a convenient swimming pool, weekly Bingo games, eating at the country club, and potlucks at a smaller village clubhouse, to name a few. They attended a nearby Clearwater Presbyterian church. They had several friends to enjoy the life they had. This was all comforting to learn that they weren't in need of a place to live, which I hadn't given thought to either before the call! As I shared with mother that I lived in the house I inherited from my father and stepmother, they learned I too didn't need a place to live. That was probably reassuring for them as well.

Limited "Parental" Experience ...

I was the only child mother could ever have. When I asked her if she really wanted me, as I had been told she didn't, and that she had even tried to kill me, she said, "Honey, I had two surgeries just to have you! There is no way I would have wanted to get rid of you or couldn't have wanted you." This made me feel better about being wanted. It made me sad though for her to never be able to have another child.

She and Bill were godparents to Andrew, who lives in Tallahassee with a family of his own. Andrew's parents were good friends of mother and Bill. Andrew's father was actually mother's first boss in banking, at Gulf to Bay Bank in 1965 and is still a good friend today. So, I also learned they had the ability to make and keep good friendships, besides being described as "wonderful godparents."

Bill had a daughter named, Karyn Wallace. Mother was a stepmother to Karyn from about 8 years old, until Karyn's untimely death from cancer at age 36. Karyn would come to visit her father and "Aunt Norm" from out of state, staying a week or two at a time. According to Carol, a good friend of Karyn's, the love I missed "was showered on Karyn." Carol recently told me that mother had "a tremendously good influence on Karyn," and that Karyn believed Aunt Norm "would have been a wonderful mother, because she was such a wonderful stepmother," and urged her to be in touch with me. However, believing I had rejected her, mother insisted I needed to be the one to contact her if I chose. With this testimonial of being "a wonderful stepmother," I trust what mother told me in our first conversation that being an abusive stepmother, like I had, was neither necessary nor acceptable.

The abuse I suffered would haunt mother. She thought all those years that at least I was having a good life apart from her. During our initial conversation, anger and disappointment filled her heart as she learned that was not the case.

With this introductory call, mother at 71 years old, and Bill at 73, had an opportunity to be "parents" again! They laughed about that. But Norma became "Mom" and Bill became my step-dad. I wasn't sure what to call Bill so I asked him what he'd prefer. He said I could call him anything I was comfortable with. I told Bill I didn't want to try to take his daughter's place. He countered with, "It's too late. God gave you to me as my daughter now!" So, I chose to call him "Dad." I think he really liked that.

What Happens Next? ...

Mother asked for my telephone number and address, and I too needed her address. Mother suggested we take it slowly, but keep in touch.

I had hoped to meet her in the not-too-distant future, but didn't speak of that during this first call. In fact, her wanting to take it slowly caused me some doubts still that she might believe our continuing this relationship would be too hurtful and painful. I still feared rejection.

I had learned much, but needed to sleep on it all a few days. My journal notes indicate I was going through an amazing spectrum of emotions:

- From concern that my family will not be understanding, to wanting to see Mom right away.
- From guilt to be doing this at all, to glad finally for the truth.
- From disappointment from all the lies, to glad she's alive.
- From just having buried one Mom, to unsure how close I want these new family ties.
- From caution about things going too fast, to wanting to change plans and head to Florida!
- From sadness over the lost years, to thankful that the Lord is apparently opening a new chapter.
- From sadness about what all this has cost her in lost years, regret and unhappiness, to uncertainty about how to get this new acquaintance started ... and not really wanting another Mom to have too close too soon.

Whatever was right or wrong about the past, I had been instructed by God to NOT judge anymore. To do that, I had to be careful to not judge whatever circumstances or situations mother shared with me as we got to know more about each other. I had also been told to, "not focus on the past, at what I'd given up, but look to the future at what I'd been given." I knew that was the next step.

Success So Soon or At Last?? ...

I called friends and Beverly the night of February 9, 1997, to let them know that I had spoken with my birth mother! They were very pleased and also surprised at how quickly I had found her once the search began.

From January 9, 1997 to February 9, 1997 ... just 30 days for a successful result!

It sometimes takes years to locate a lost loved one. However, looking at it another way: the search to find Mom did take a lifetime:

For me, her absence was from 5 years old to almost 50.

For Mom, my absence was from 26 years old to 71.

45 years missed in both of our lives.

In God's timetable, 45 years is just a blink; but for us it was a lifetime. While the "search" is over ... the relationship is just beginning!

Chapter 3

REUNION TIME

*"For God hath not given us the spirit of fear,
but of power, and of love, and of a sound mind."*
II Timothy 1:7

I thought I needed to sleep a few nights on what I'd learned in my very first conversation with Mom; but I didn't even need one night sleeping on it!

I'd had 45 years of sleeping on my past life and needed to get on with the life I'd been given! Some HOT "TO DOs" came to mind right away:

First, I wrote Mom a note and mailed it with a picture of Cricket and me - I figured she needed to know what I looked like, as well as her new "4-legged grandkid"! I asked Mom in the note to send me a picture of her.

Secondly, sleep was fretful that night thinking about what I'd learned and how to proceed. I decided to make some plans to go meet her. Well, it wasn't actually *meeting* her; it was seeing her again. But since I didn't remember anything about her, it was like a brand new meeting for me!

Then, I thought what better time than to meet on my 50th birthday, which was only two weeks away!

But the "What ifs" attacked again!

What if she didn't want to meet me?

What if I couldn't get her to invite me to her house to meet?

What if it was too soon for a meeting? Was it presumptuous to want one?

What if she thought it was too painful to get together?

Starting Our New Life! ...

Eventually, I fell asleep the night of February 9, 1997, but awakened early on February 10. A new life lay ahead and I'd better get it started!

I decided to call Mom and say "Hi Mom!" since she hadn't heard that for 45 years - or maybe never. Being only 5 years old when she last saw me, I was probably still calling her "Mommy" back then.

She answered my call right away. I said, "Hi Mom!"

She sounded really happy to hear from me, and again said, "Hi Sweetheart!"

The Bible verse in I Peter 1:8 talks about "rejoicing with joy unspeakable," but I never understood the phrase until that moment. It truly was an "Ah-Ha" moment! I had a swelling of joy inside me that was indescribable! To actually have my mother genuinely happy to hear from me - WOW! I also recalled from the night before that she had said she "truly loved me," after thinking she didn't for all those years. My heart finally felt filled up! Her love must have been the missing piece in my heart! That's what "joy unspeakable" felt like! What joy a mother's love could bring - and it was only the beginning!

We talked briefly before I went to work. She said she had already put a note in the mail to me, along with a picture of herself and Dad. I told her I had done likewise! This was the first sign, of many to come, that we thought very much alike! What another joyous experience that was ... after living my whole life with people who were often hard to relate to!

Mom said she had hardly slept the previous night because she was so excited to hear from me. Something else we had in common!

I told her I would call her that evening. But before we said "Good-bye," she said, "Remember that I love you very much."

Hesitantly, I said, "Maybe some day I can learn to do the same."

After 45 years, one doesn't just instantly say, "Hi Mom! I love you!" I didn't even know this woman. It was going to take time to learn to love her and to learn to trust her; to find out who she really was and where I fit in her life; and to learn to trust myself. I knew I had to make the journey. I just needed to do it in small steps. Mom had the benefit of loving me for those 45 years I was missing; I had to start from scratch.

Sharing the News with Others ...

I shared the exciting news at work about actually speaking with my birth mother the previous night. Those who knew the many steps of my journey to find her were very happy for me. They found the story very interesting, including the miracles and leading of God along the way. Later, they shared that they were more than just happy for me; but were also cautiously optimistic, as they didn't want to see me hurt again.

They started asking when I was going to meet her. I told them I was waiting for her letter that was in the mail before thinking of making travel plans. I would be talking with her more during this week before deciding to visit or not. In checking the travel schedule, however, I did see that I could have available days off around my birthday.

When I spoke with my friend, Kaye, who was planning my 50th birthday party, about having found my birth mother, she was thrilled for me and totally understood that I might be going to meet Mom on my birthday. So, party plans were delayed. For a long time I was envious of the relationship Kaye had with her children, wondering if they knew how special their mother was, how understanding, how interested in their lives. Often I had wished Kaye had been my mother; but settled for her very dear friendship that has lasted over 35 years. God knew I needed an understanding friend to help me cope along the way. Kaye was that kind of person and a good Christian friend.

Again, I was hesitant to share the actual news of finding my birth mother with my half-brother. If I told him, an explanation would be needed about other people now becoming part of our lives as new family members. I wasn't sure how he would take that news; so, I delayed telling him for now.

"Getting Acquainted" with Uncertainties ...

On Tuesday, February 11, my journal reflects I felt like I was still on a "wild roller coaster ride!"

Mom called me early in the morning wanting to "schedule an appointment" to talk with me after work. She didn't elaborate about the topic for discussion. That made me nervous and suspicious. I was still very "gun-shy" about whether our connection was too painful for Mom to handle and thought maybe she wanted to tell me she didn't want our relationship to go further.

I was upset all day wondering why she wanted to talk, especially frightened she would say this evening's call would be our last one. I was so anxious I couldn't even eat dinner that evening.

You might wonder why I didn't just call her back and ask her the topic of the evening's discussion. But I felt I was still "walking on eggshells" with her and didn't want to push the relationship faster than she was willing to go.

I reflected about our morning conversation, trying to reason it out. After asking for an appointment time in the evening to talk, she went on to ask me how I liked my job. That seemed like a safe topic, so I didn't think she wanted to discuss that further.

I was busy thinking about my concerns, so I didn't have any idea what was concerning Mom. I was trying not to judge my stepmother and father for their choices; trying to fathom what Mom's life had been like for my 45-year absence; and trying not to be sad for the stolen years for either Mom or me.

Besides, Mom told me she loved me before she got off the call again this morning … so why should I have doubts about what she wanted to discuss that night? I've heard that she loves me more in 3 days than I have in probably 30 years! It feels good! And maybe that's the reason for my uncertainty: I don't want to believe she doesn't want to continue getting acquainted, now that I've found her.

Mystery Solved … with Surprising Results! …

Her call came that evening, right at the scheduled time. Mystery solved!

Mom was just being courteous about reserving certain times during the week for us to talk. She had no idea, and I didn't tell her for a long time, that she had made me so nervous when she asked to schedule an appointment to talk with me.

There were three topics on Mom's mind:

She wanted to keep getting to know each other, but was sensitive to my work schedule.

The 3-hour time difference between Florida and California made it a little difficult for us to be able to have those talks at decent hours. So, she was trying to figure out the best times for both of us to connect.

Get ready for this 'talking point': Mom also wanted for us "to think about how to meet."

Hooray!! Didn't that last point play right into what I had been thinking!

Mom mentioned that she "couldn't wait until May" when they would be vacationing on the West Coast for us to meet because "that was too long to wait." She did consider the possibility of us meeting in Reno, near to where she knew my nieces lived. But again, she said May was too long to wait. Now that made me a pretty happy "kid!!"

I hadn't told her my thoughts about visiting Florida sooner than she was proposing we meet. So, I risked jumping out there with: "How about a week from Friday?"

It quickly became obvious that the furthest thing from her mind was my coming East to meet her. Consequently, my question sort of went over her head at that point. She started talking about her "having a doctor's appointment on that Friday."

Not immediately realizing she didn't catch on to my idea of coming East, I'm thinking, "Geez, I'm coming all the way to Florida after 45 years, so I would think she could possibly cancel or reschedule her appointment!" But then thought, "Maybe it's for something serious, so I'd better not say anything like that."

So, in my usual 'problem-solving way,' I countered with: "Well, if you could give me directions and your address, I could rent a car, get a map, find my way to your place. I could try to time my flight so I would arrive around the time you'd get back from your doctor's appointment."

It was momentarily quiet on her end of the call. Suddenly, the light went on! She said very excitedly, "Are you coming here?!"

I was excited that she was excited! Yet I responded guardedly, "Yes, I thought I would, if that's okay with you."

Without responding to my comment, she then clarified, "Are you going to be here on your birthday?!"

I like to surprise people; so, I was thrilled thinking she recognized the surprise that I had planned: to be there for my birthday. However, it turned out the reason she asked the question was because she had already ordered a dozen long-stemmed red roses to be delivered to my office on my birthday! So, she was thinking about having to change those plans, when all of a sudden the whole prospect of us meeting in less than ten days dawned on her! Then, she was elated! I heard Mom share the news quickly with Dad; then, continued conversing with me.

Later, Mom would tell me Dad was happy about my prospective visit too. Dad wanted whatever made Mom happy. But at that point in our relationship, I wasn't anymore confident about Dad's acceptance of me than I was about Mom's. However, I did respect that they had been married for over 40 years and, since I was just on the scene, getting along with Dad was as important as solidifying my relationship with Mom. So I was hopeful it would all work out. I breathed a prayer that God would make it all right … and kept going.

Mom told me when she ordered the flowers that the florist was excited to hear the reason for the order. The florist actually offered to arrange for the newspapers and cameras if we physically reunited sometime in the future. Mom quickly told her "No way! This is private." I hadn't really given that any thought yet, but decided I rather liked the private approach too. With all of the emotions and hurts involved in this particular reunion, I agreed that privacy in our reunion would be best.

However, Mom was quick to tell me that she and Dad "wanted to meet my flight," so she would have "to move her doctor's appointment" and added, "which would be no problem!" That was encouraging to me, as it wasn't a doctor's appointment for anything serious. Plus, that's a Mom wanting to see "her kid!"

Following this second day in our new relationship, I realize I've learned a few more ways Mom and I are alike: she follows through on what she says (she called promptly at 6:30 to have our scheduled talk). Mom is thoughtful (roses were on order already; however, I did tell her after I learned about the roses that I'm allergic to them; so, she quickly made a note of that unknown fact to remember for future reference). She keeps lists of TO DOs; has a good sense of humor; tries to find the good in a situation or person; and reads her Bible every day.

Making Trip Plans …

I started to make trip plans as soon as we got off the phone. I booked the flights after I arrived at work. I had no miles banked for a free ticket so must pay full fare. But this is one flight I must make, whether I can afford it or not! Who would have ever believed that I would finally be meeting her?! What an unbelievable turnaround in my thinking, because of Beverly's guidance, God's leading, and lessons learned in not judging and in forgiveness.

I asked my friend, Pat, to make up another plaque of the saying that God gave me on January 9, 1997:

**"Don't focus on the past, at what you've given up,
but look to the future at what you've been given."**

I wanted to give one to Mom when we meet and keep one for myself.

The in-person reunion is now scheduled for February 21-24, 1997. My plane is scheduled to land in Tampa, Florida, and Mom and I will actually reunite, ironically, on my father's birthday, February 21! That's just the way the trip and my work schedule allowed. There honestly was no "So there!" intended!

When I shared with my co-workers that the reunion had been scheduled, they were truly excited for me. People who had encouraged me were great supporters.

Every time I relay the story, it gets easier to accept. I am overwhelmed, often to tears, when I think of God's leading in this whole life-changing event. To think God loves Mom and me enough to do this ... in His way and His timing. It is a humbling experience as well as very emotional.

I had a Valentine's Day bouquet ordered for Mom and Dad; also, a "thank you" bouquet for Aunt Phyllis and one for Uncle Rich, for their part in helping to right this wrong in Mom's and my lives.

A Special Card and Signature...

On February 12, Mom called me again in the morning. Momentarily, I held my breath and thought she was going to say that she didn't want to go forward with our relationship. Then, she said, "I love you very much."

I heard the happiness and love in her voice. I started to believe that I'd keep hearing from her.

I wrote and mailed Mom a "thinking of you" card after talking with her. It was prompted by a devotional from a copy of *"Daily Bread"* entitled, "Thanks for Inconvenience." The devotional concludes with this statement, "If you're enduring a long-term inconvenience, consider thanking God for what He has taught you through it." The irony is this devotional is dated December 20 and it is now February 12 of the following year. I read the "Daily Bread" a few months in arrears, loaning the more current months to other people. It always amazes me when the one I read for the day seems like it is written just for me!

In the "thinking of you" card, I finally admit that every time I hear Mom's voice say "Hello," I am filled with momentary fear that she's not going to be able to continue our relationship due to the hurt it surfaces. But I go on to say, when she starts talking, the happiness and love come through and the fear of rejection subsides.

I thank her for her love, in spite of the circumstances. I tell her I'm so overwhelmed by the thoughts of what she has gone through, yet am blessed by what I see as her spirit of "instant forgiveness." I write that I'm overwhelmed with gratitude she loved me all those years, instead of what I was told all my life.

I mention it is remarkable, in spite of all the bitterness and sadness we've felt for 45 years, that we share the bond of our love for the Lord; that our reunion would be so different if we both weren't Christians; that I thank God He saved us both. I share with Mom that I keep telling people what God is doing to restore my joy - which has been gone for so long.

I tell Mom I love the way she responds to things, being so positive and upbeat, versus the critical spirit that used to surround me and made me so weary. I thank her for wanting to go forward and not look back. I admit that I'm not quite there yet, although I realize this is a 45-year lesson in love and forgiveness. I tell her I pray for her daily and thank God that He let her live so this wrong can be righted in-person.

I close with the statement that I'm looking forward to February 21 and each time we speak. For the first time, I sign it, "Love, Jan."

I asked God to take away my anger, but I guess I'm still grieving over what I learned.

However, it is such an overwhelming feeling to be loved with a mother's unconditional love! A mother's love seems to parallel how God loves us … no matter what has happened, for whatever reasons, God's love never ends. It appears this is a lesson I will keep learning about my mother's love too.

Another thing I realized today is that this mother-daughter relationship, which is starting with the basics, is not an adult-child situation. I can observe it through adult eyes and appreciate her wisdom and responses more.

Another Daily Dose of Getting Acquainted …

Mom had several reasons for calling me this morning. One was to tell me that she moved her doctor appointment and the flower delivery. She said she didn't want to embarrass me by sending the flowers to work, as she wasn't sure if I told anyone.

I replied, "Anyone?? I've told EVERYONE!"

So, she decided she's changing the order again for them to go to work!

Mom also said that she and Dad want me to stay with them, but I have to sleep on the couch. It seems the spare room holds many of her collection of 486 Teddy Bears! Isn't that interesting! Guess what I was taking to her next Friday - yep, number 487! At least it's bound to be loved! I understand a penchant to collect things, since I collect sea otters and lighthouses. But there must be an interesting story behind 486 of any one thing! I'll have to be sure to ask when we meet.

She was worried about what foods to serve when I'm there. She realized we have to start at the beginning and figure everything out. They want to take me to the "best steakhouse in the world!" Dad agreed with that, when she told him to get on the phone too. He said he's very happy we'll be able to enjoy the time together.

Mom even offered for me to borrow some of her clothes when I come to visit. In my mind, I know she's not a "bag lady" - but I have no clue what taste she has in clothing versus my tastes. So, I'm quickly back-pedaling with the story about why I don't like to borrow things from people. Once I borrowed an Al Martino Cassette Tape to play in my car from someone at work, only to have it unravel in my tape player. I was never able to replace the exact Cassette; it was out of stock. (True story!) I vowed then to never borrow from someone else. She gave in at that point, but explained she was just offering so I didn't have to carry the extra weight in my suitcases. A kind and thoughtful offer by her - but I wasn't ready to try a mother-daughter clothing exchange yet.

It's really difficult to concentrate on work with this incredible saga unfolding. I confirmed my tickets for the February trip to meet Mom and Dad. I also arranged for my March vacation and business travels to include a stopover in Ohio to see Uncle Rich and Aunt Phyllis, Mom's sister.

Chasing the Mailman ...
At noon, I left work and drove around my neighborhood trying to track

down the mailman. I only lived three miles from the office, so it wasn't a long trip. But it seemed to me that Mom's letter, mailed two days ago with her picture, should be arriving - and I couldn't wait until after work to check the mail. Jesse has been my mailman for many years, so he recognized my car, else he might have thought I was trying to carjack his mail truck!

I explained that I "found my birth mother and have been waiting 45 years to hear from her, but can't wait one more hour to see if her letter arrived." He patiently checked to see if it was in my stack of mail. No letter yet, unfortunately! I thanked him for his trouble and said I'd check again later in the week. I think he knew "later in the week" translated into "tomorrow!"

Breaking the News to my Half-Brother ...

After getting enough courage and advice, I called my sister-in-law and asked for the telephone numbers where my half-brother was staying during his current business trip. I wanted to speak with him as soon as possible. As usual, my sister-in-law was excited and happy for me as I told her about connecting with my mother.

I called my half-brother later that night. After listening to his work problems, I shared with him what has been happening in my life, about finding Mom and the plans to go see her. He took the news better than I expected.

Although trying to not sound negative, he did question if I was sure I could handle this: after just burying one mother, was I ready for another?

I responded positively, "God appears to have given me a healthy one ... and who knows, maybe she'll take care of me!" I added, "the only thing I know is that God is guiding this whole process and I need to obey."

Hearing from Mom Tonight ...

I am tired from emotional strain and crying so much; but was real excited when I got home from dinner out to hear a message from Mom on my answering machine. She wanted to thank me for the Valentine's Bouquet.

I saved her message and replayed it a few times. It made me feel good. I like hearing her voice.

When I tried to return her call, the line was busy. It was getting too late to call Florida, so I vowed to call her in the morning.

At least Mom doesn't yell at me for coming home late. She's also considerate to not call me at work, as she didn't like it when she worked and employees took personal calls. The contrast to my stepmother goes on!

Interesting Insights from our Growing Relationship ...

For February 13, my journal says, "WOW! What an emotional day - again! This incredible journey goes on."

First thing this morning I called Mom to acknowledge her call from last night. I told her the letter and picture didn't come. She laughed that I tracked down the mailman!

I shared with her my momentary fear that when she calls, it's going to be too painful for her to keep contacting me and continuing to develop our relationship. She said I'd "better get used to her because she intends to be around a long time." Now that she's "got me," she's "not letting go!" Boy, does that feel good!!

Conversations with her are enjoyable, and I find myself reluctant to get off the phone. She's interested in me, considerate, very happy, thinks a lot like me - although tells it straight forward better than me. Most importantly, she loves me.

I told Mom I don't want to do anything that will hurt her. I like her very much, but I'm not sure I love her yet. I know she loves me because of her motherly unconditional love; but I don't think I can turn on my love that automatically or this soon. She was wonderful about it; she said, "It will take time." She said she loves me because she gave birth to me and she'd be happy if I just liked her.

I admitted I did already like her. But had been made to love my stepmother, so I'm not sure I knew what genuine love was between a mother and daughter. I needed to experience that type of love before I would be able to recognize and embrace it. My prayer was for my love to grow, since God seems to have orchestrated all this so perfectly.

It was a relief for me to be able to discuss this concern with Mom and to have her be so understanding. She may have been very hurt by my honesty, but she never let me know if she was.

Mom said she and Dad were trying to organize some special things. She asked if I wanted to go to church with them Sunday, and I said "Sure!"

She asked me all of the questions about what I like to eat ... starting with "Do you like peanut butter?" It seems basic. But we know nothing about each other's likes and dislikes, except what we've had a chance to discuss in the past three days. She says she is taking notes each time we talk, so she doesn't forget things I like and dislike. I too take notes of things to be remembered for future reference.

She is so easy to talk to and I want to talk with her. I still hesitate about letting her get off the phone. I feel like I can talk with her about anything and she's interested in what I have to say. She never rushes the conversation, except that she doesn't want me to be late for work.

She admits she is so nervous about our reunion that she is hardly eating. Likewise, I forgot to eat dinner tonight and even forgot where I parked my car after work! So, who is more nervous?!

Mom shared with me that two baby pictures of me fell out of her Bible in her closet about two weeks prior to my contacting her.

I said, "Wasn't that amazing! Like God was preparing you for my contacting you! That is wonderful, I'd love to see the pictures."

"They got thrown away," she sadly said, "like all of the other painful reminders, as we were cleaning out the closet."

So, I tried to cheer her up with, "Well, we'll just have to take some more photos and make some new memories, when I come to visit next week!"

Mom agreed.

The Letter and Pictures Arrived ...

I chased the mailman down again today, and this time he had the letter! I didn't even get back in my car before I tore open the envelope. The letter was very special. But then I looked at the pictures and panicked. I thought, "Who is this woman?!"

Suddenly, I realized there is a new stage to go through. This lady doesn't look like my mother when I view the picture. The only mind picture I have is of my stepmother for 45 years as my mother. I had no clue what my birth mother would look like. What if I can't relate to this lady who is my mother and what if I am not able to instantly love her like she loves me? There are those "What ifs" again!!

Quickly, I page my therapist! Beverly is standing on the dock ready to board the boat to Catalina Island and returns my call, wondering what is wrong.

I say, "I just got this picture of my mother and I don't know who she is!

How am I going to be able to love her back like she loves me??"

Calmly, Beverly says, "Jan, calm down. Just go look in the mirror and imagine yourself 20 years from now. That's who she is. It's going to be all right. Just take it slowly. Just let the love grow gradually."

I said something brilliant like, "Oh, okay." I thanked her for taking my call, and raced home to look in the mirror!

When I got home and took a good look in that mirror, Beverly was right again. That lady's picture is me in 20 years! I just needed to get used to visualizing that.

This is another example of when "the obvious isn't always obvious" to someone too close to the situation. But my counselor, in my corner, once again knew how to help me through this crisis and get on to the next level of understanding.

Here's what my Mom's letter said ... the **first one I've ever had** from her:

2/10/97

Hi Honey:

> This becoming a mother at 71 isn't easy. But at least I skipped the morning sickness this time. I had 2 surgeries and a difficult 9 months to have you ... but you were worth every bit of it!

> You were loved by my folks as well as me – and spent a lot of time with them because of your getting every blessed germ your Uncle Rich brought home from school.

> I dreamed so many times of the phone call that came last night. When I got up this morning I realized it was "for real!" (Didn't get much sleep, however!)

> Our best bet now is to get used to our new family circle. Dad asked if I wanted to fly out to see you – after all the years we flew, I am uneasy in a plane. So we take road trips. (More about that later.)

> My bad days were always Mother's Day and the whole month of February – but you've changed all that. We'll just celebrate 2/9 as our special day and go from there.

> I love you and neither time nor distance will ever change that. I always have been and will always be your   - Mom -

Wow! Isn't this special!!

An Important Weekend Getaway ...

Everybody is very happy for me about this upcoming reunion. They say I look happier already!

Mom says all of her friends are happy for her too.

I forget it's only been four days since Mom and I were reunited and so much has happened so fast. This is an event that seems almost incredible and certainly is life-changing. It's no wonder I'm emotionally drained and still mixed up.

Maybe this weekend's previously scheduled getaway, February 14 -17, to a Northern California Christian Singles Conference will help me clear my head and sort out all that's going on in my heart.

I planned to call Mom and Dad from along the way, so they wouldn't worry about me. Besides, talking with them daily was an important part of this growing relationship for me.

The Conference gave me time to organize my thoughts and feelings. The speakers focused on very timely topics for my situation such as, "Set Free to Be All You Can Be," "Hope Through Hard Times," and "Discovering God's Will for Our Lives." In the session, "Tests We Have to Face," the two sub-topics were: "Waiting for Suffering to Pass" and "Loving Our Enemies." How appropriate were all of these?! I know there were lots of other campers present, but the Lord sure seemed to have prepared much of the program to assist me.

While at the Conference, I took time to journal "How Do I Feel Now?" and some of those thoughts are interesting in retrospect:

- I don't want to ever hurt Mom or let her be hurt again.
- I want to get to know her more. She and Dad must be very special people to have a love that endured for 44 years so far.
- It's okay with Mom if I just like her; she hopes I can grow to love her; but the pressure's eased for me that she recognizes it will take me some time.
- I'm scared a bit by how different life will be going forward; life will never be the same; new challenges lie ahead.
- I need to take things one day at a time! This elephant's too big; need to experience it in little chunks and savor each one.
- Feels like my grieving over my stepmother is over.

- Feels like I'm now grieving for Mom over what she lost, but know I can't make up for it; we can both only enjoy what time we have left together; God must REALLY think she's special to have let her endure this pain for all those years!
- I'm assured Mom's NOT going to leave me; she wants to stay in my life.
- As adult-to-adult, I can experience a mother-daughter relationship with an ability to comprehend and appreciate her and what she does and says; that's very different from growing up with her.
- I have an opportunity that not many people EVER have; not sure what God wants us to do with this unique story or situation, but need to let Him lead … not me!
- I don't want to disappoint Mom and Dad when we meet; feels like there are some high expectations; hope everything's going to be great when we meet.

Three Bible stories came to mind that related to Mom's and my years of separation:

The Israelites wandered in the wilderness for 40 years - our wanderings lasted 45 years. Either number you look at is a long time!

King Solomon made the decision to split the child in two, to test who the real mother was - my real mother eventually gave me up, rather than have me more upset with trying to balance between two mothers in my life.

Joseph eventually was promoted to Pharaoh's Court, but must have wondered, "Why did I have to endure all the years of bondage?" - after 45 years of "bondage," Mom and I are now "in Pharaoh's Court," to enjoy our new lives together.

Before the Conference ended, God had already used the story of our trials and reunion plan in several ways:

A Northern California Youth Director who heard my story wanted permission to share it with his kids at church.

The same Youth Director told many of the campers the story and said it was a highlight for him of this weekend's Conference.

My friend's husband was using what God told me on January 9, 1997:

"Don't focus on the past, at what you've given up,
but look to the future at what you've been given."

… as a birthday gift for graduates of his counseling program.

During a closing time of meditation, two Psalms came to my mind. I made notations of what healing, comforting thoughts God gave me that day:

> Thoughts about Psalm 139:
> "God knew me before I was born, and knew what was going to happen, but He's been with me all the way. He knows how hurt Mom's been, but God has comforted her and the future will be sweeter than all of the past was hard. I can love her as He helps me, just as He loves me as a child of His. This weekend is one of preparation for the rest of my life."

> Thoughts about Psalm 23:
> "I am your Shepherd and will do only what is good for you, my child."

The Conference was a very refreshing time for me. A "mountaintop" getaway experience is helpful to handle the real "valleys" of life. This time was no exception and certainly had to be God's timing yet again for me!

I called Mom and Dad from the Conference to keep them updated on its progress, as well as to check how they were doing.

On February 17, I called again upon my return home. I thanked them for the 2-foot tall Valentine card! It was "For a Wonderful Daughter, Janet Gayle" … and was signed with "Lots of Love, Mom!" It really felt good.

Reunion Trip Preparations … in Florida

Both Mom and Dad were excited about my coming to Florida in just four days! They had been having some busy times on their end in preparation for the visit.

Some of their dearest friends and Mom's church never knew I existed. Mom wanted to prepare these people for my upcoming visit so I wouldn't be embarrassed to meet them. I didn't even think about how it would appear to folks who didn't know Mom had a daughter almost 50 years old! They thought she was childless all those years.

She approached the minister of her Presbyterian church and asked if she could say a few words to the congregation on the Sunday before I would be attending. She explained to the congregation that I was coming to visit. She told them I had contacted her after 45 years. She emphasized I wasn't illegitimate, just not in touch all those years due to unfortunate issues related to being kidnapped from her when I was 5 years old. She discussed her efforts to find me; and how I finally got the message from the Lord to seek her out. The congregation was in tears before Mom got half way through the talk. The minister only interrupted once to say, "Ah-ha! That's why you wouldn't come to church on Mother's Day!" So, the church was prepared for my attendance, and my mother felt that she had protected me from anyone possibly speculating about where I came from. Mom later told me that was the first time she had ever spoken publicly at church. What a testimony for one's first speech!

Mom and Dad took their long-time friends, Carl and Jane, to dinner and explained about my existence. They were shocked. Actually, Mom's words in a card to me were:

> "I showed them your picture and picked them up off the floor. They just couldn't believe I had a daughter. So it shows I can keep a secret. They remembered how I used to skip Mother's Day affairs and now know why."

But Carl and Jane were happy for Mom, and wanted to meet me on an upcoming visit, when possible. Andrew, Carl and Jane's son who is Mom and Dad's godson, wanted to be included too when his schedule permitted.

Carol was another person who was very close to Mom and Dad, but knew very little about me. Carol was my step-dad's daughter's best friend and maintained a close relationship with Mom and Dad after Dad's daughter died of cancer at 36. Carol called Mom and Dad "Aunt Norm" and "Uncle Bill," and Mom and Dad treated her extra special. Carol also wanted to meet me during an upcoming visit.

Carol's birthday is two days after mine. Carol and Karyn were close in age to me. So, at least Mom and Dad had some people in their lives who helped take my place during the years of my absence.

Recently, Carol shared with me that Mom and Dad told her they were facing my upcoming visit with some trepidation, but were looking forward to it. They felt it was important that Carol and I get along, but were concerned we wouldn't like each other. After we did get together, Mom and Dad continued to be concerned that they treat Carol and me the same, even though I was their daughter.

Carol had heard about me from Dad's daughter, Karyn, who had told Carol she and I used to play together at church. I didn't remember that at all.

During the 25-year relationship Mom and Dad had with Carol to this reunion point, Carol only remembered two conversations about me with Mom, both were brief and several years earlier. The last time, Carol had urged Mom to contact me saying, "If she knew you, I know she'd love you." But Mom said when I turned 21 and could have been free to contact her, I didn't. Consequently, Mom felt she should give up hope of any contact. Mom chose not to initiate the contact because she felt it should be mine to do if I wanted to after I became an adult. Mom didn't want to take the chance of my rejection of her and the subsequent hurt.

Reunion Trip Preparations … in California

I spent time gathering up some photos and old school mementos to share with Mom as some glimpses of my life that she missed. I even had Valentines from when I was in grade school! No wonder I never got rid of them, it must have been important to save these to share with Mom!

On Tuesday, February 18, I called Mom in the morning and again that night. We spoke long and easily both times. We're both excited about Friday! I need to think of something to take Dad … maybe an answering machine. I have Teddy Bear # 487 for Mom … he is named "Honey Bear," holding a honey pot with honey dripping all over him!

Friends I spoke with tonight are very happy for Mom and me.

On a sad note, Cricket isn't doing well again; I had to increase her medicines.

On Wednesday, February 19, I had a therapy session with Beverly, to keep my head on straight about this reunion.

I called Mom when I got home from work. She is getting nervous about the possibility that I might not like her. I told her, "God didn't bring us together for that to happen." She offered that I could ask her anything I want to when we meet or in any conversation we have.

I called more friends with this marvelous story and where I was going on Friday. My sister-in-law and my stepmother's brother, Uncle Walt, called to wish me luck and tell me they are happy for me.

Thursday, February 20, started with a call from Mom. Now she must be suffering from the "What ifs!" She's very nervous, thinking that I won't like her. I told her "NO WAY!" I already like her very much and God assured me He's going to help me love her. I reassured her, "God didn't bring us this far for it not to work out. So, don't worry about it."

Everything at work fell into place for me to be gone these few important days as planned.

Cricket was staying overnight at the vet's; my dog-sitter would pick her up tomorrow.

That night I packed and got ready for an early limo pick up. I had an early flight from Los Angeles International airport to Tampa with a brief stopover in Denver.

It was time to see my mother for the first time in 45 years! I could hardly wait!

Reunion Day, February 21, 1997 ...

The flight left timely, but couldn't fly fast enough to suit me!

At the check-in counter, I learned I had enough miles banked with United Airlines to upgrade to First Class. That was an unexpected bonus on this trip! I felt good that I'd be able to get off the plane quickly once we got to Tampa.

During the stopover flight in Denver, I deplaned and called Mom to tell her, "I'm almost there!"

She said, "Will you hurry up!!" We both laughed!

I told her, "I'm looking forward to seeing you both!" She and Dad agreed they could hardly wait to meet me!

She told me Dad would be there to take our picture. Mom was wearing the same outfit that she had on in the first picture she sent me ... so I'd recognize her. I told her what I was wearing so she'd recognize me too and Dad could get the picture at the reunion moment!

I got back on the plane ... calm again; everything was going fine. Oops! I just discovered I left my purse at the telephone in the airport terminal! Who was nervous?? Not me!!

So, I raced off the plane; miraculously found my purse where I left it; and got back on board! This was one connecting flight I sure didn't want to miss!

As I started to take my seat, I noticed there was a man to my left now. What I didn't notice until we were going to land in Tampa was that the man next to me was a paraplegic and looked like he would be the last one off the flight. Wouldn't you know it on the flight where time was of the essence to me! But I realized at least I could walk off the plane on my own, and should be grateful for that. So, I would just have to be patient.

Poor Mom and Dad would be waiting - with Dad holding a camera the whole time deplaning was in process, hoping for that special reunion photo. I didn't have any way to tell them I would be off as one of the last passengers!

As we taxied into Tampa, my heart started beating faster. Now I was starting to get more nervous. But the reunion was definitely going to happen, so I prepared to deplane.

As I got up the jet way, I started looking for my mother's outfit from the picture. I thought I'd remember it. The people in front of me seemed to split off to the right and the left, just as I exited the jet way. That's because Mom was standing there, as close as she could to the jet way opening.

There she was with her arms opened to greet me. Her hug felt good. She said, "Hi Baby! It's so good to see you finally!"

Then, she said, "turn toward the camera." Just then a man, who was oblivious to our special moment, moved between Dad's camera and us! So, we had a great reunion photo of this man whose name we didn't know! But many more photos followed to capture this once-in-a-lifetime moment.

Then, I was introduced to Dad. He was a very tall, big man, but gave me a gentle hug too. I later learned someone nicknamed him "the gentle giant," a name that fit him well.

We reclaimed the baggage and headed to the car they have named "Big Red!" It was a beautiful Lincoln Towncar, red on the bottom, with a white half vinyl roof. Dad was driving ... but Mom wanted to get in the back with me, so we could hold hands and talk better on the drive to their condominium.

Her wanting to sit close to me and hold my hand felt very special. We did that a lot during reunion weekend. Her touch was special and memorable for me. Apparently it felt good to her too.

When we would sit in the living room watching TV at times this weekend and during future visits, I'd sit at the base of her chair with her hand on my shoulder and my hand over her hand. Here I was almost 50 years old but I couldn't get enough of her touch, after 45 years of not knowing it.

Cove Cay ... Here We Come ...

We headed out of Tampa towards Clearwater. We went over a bridge that extends above Tampa Bay. I asked where we were and I'm sure they told me. But I was so overwhelmed by this reunion event I couldn't take in all the geographic facts.

When we got near their condominium complex, I saw the sign "Cove Cay" for the first time. We drove into the complex, which is comprised of several multi-story buildings, and located their building. I noticed there is a swimming pool almost outside their front door and a small clubhouse nearby. As we entered their 1st floor unit, you looked out onto the golf course through their patio windows. We entered the living room. Behind us was their kitchen; to the right down the hall were the two bedrooms and bathrooms.

There's a table set up between the kitchen and living room that has balloons, a birthday banner, and a luscious looking pineapple upside-down cake!! Yum! Two candles, a "5" and a "0," are on the cake … guess for whose birthday?! Mom even said I "don't have to wait until my birthday to have a piece!" I liked her house rules and enjoyed an early piece of my birthday cake!

I asked if I may put my suitcases in the spare bedroom, which is when I encountered the Teddy Bear "den"! There were two white bears, almost as tall as me, plus many smaller ones sort of pushed to the edges of the room, so I could use the remaining space for the weekend! But I was not making any critical comments this weekend and jeopardizing our newly formed relationship. So, I kept any observations or questions to myself at this point.

I brought out "Honey Bear" and the plaque with God's message from January 9, 1997, and gave these "glad-to-meet-you" gifts to Mom. She gave me a Teddy Bear holding an "I Love You" heart, seated on a coffee cup with a Valentine balloon attached.

While we're up walking around, Mom started showing me the pictures displayed in the hallway. I quickly realized each of these people was very important to Mom and Dad. Still in my overwhelmed state, however, I was having trouble keeping straight who-was-who. I hope it won't be as difficult after we meet in-person! I want to impress Mom and Dad that I'm interested in their lives and the details they are sharing are important to me; but I just can't keep up with all this new information.

When we toured the kitchen, I noticed her kitchen table had a display on it … some bears and other decorations with a theme … this time it was "Valentine's Day" decor. The table was pushed right up against the kitchen window and it didn't appear they ate at the table. Mom explained she liked to change the theme in the window, and the grandkids in the complex liked to come by and see the different decorated displays Mom produces. Very creative of her and cute that she does it to pleasure others.

I inquired where they eat dinner and she told me, "On TV trays in the living room." Another novel house rule!

When we re-entered the living room, Dad was sitting in his chair, Mom took her usual chair, and I have three others to choose from. I selected a seat that looks out onto the golf course and places me across from both Mom and Dad. We started to talk, getting better acquainted. It's a bit awkward and I was definitely still nervous, though trying to appear not to be.

Dad proudly told me that everyone who meets my mother loves her. I felt like this was a strong hint that I should be able to love her too! He has Mom's banking and real estate awards mounted all over the walls of the condo. He said they could never have retired if she hadn't kept working through and after his heart attack; he said her bank retirement enabled them both to retire when they did. It's obvious he is very proud of Mom. What a special man to give his wife so much credit!

Then, Mom gave me another gift to open. It was her favorite opal and diamond ring. Wow! How generous of her! She must believe our relationship is for the long term! She told me that you never buy yourself an opal, as it's unlucky … opals are to be given as a gift. This was my first opal ever and coming from Mom, it was extra special. I wear it every day on my left hand ring finger. We are bound together for life, even if we've had a later start than desired.

We spent the rest of the day together just visiting and getting better acquainted. They looked at the pictures I brought, and I looked at pictures of their past. She didn't want to spend any time looking at pictures of my father or my stepmother, which was understandable.

What we had for dinner, I don't specifically recall, but I do know Mom is a great cook just like Dad had bragged.

I thought it was going to prove interesting trying to fit in this family when I observed Mom cutting up all of Dad's dinner into little bites to serve him! I thought, "Boy! Is he ever spoiled!" Then, I thought, "Maybe he has a chewing problem or something, so be quiet about it!" But Mom told me she just does it to make it easy for Dad.

I quickly learned that Dad spoils Mom too! Anything she wants to make her happy or that she needs, he wants her to have. He told me I was "the only thing" in all of the years they have been together that he couldn't give her "to make her happy." That really bothered him all those years; so, he is very glad

I'm on the scene now.

Reflections on Our First Day Reunited ...

After Mom and Dad went to bed, I spent time thinking, crying, and praying. The emotions overwhelmed me. When I'm tired, I'm more vulnerable and this was one of those times. The reunion day went well, but I had lots of thoughts and feelings running through my mind.

I got a little sleep, but a bad dream woke me up. So, I got up and started to journal what was on my mind.

First of all, I already know I am growing to love Mom ... and Dad. They love each other very much and I'm VERY GLAD to see that. They respect each other; she looks after his needs, he worries about her and her needs. They know how to laugh together. It's great to see how happy they are because of each other.

The sadness I feel, and cry about now, is for two reasons: the stolen years and the incredible ability Mom has to forgive and go on. I know I can't recover those lost years, but I feel sad that my stepmother and father lied so much, let me believe Mom was a bad person, and I believed them all those years ... 45 years is so long to pay a price like Mom paid. My tears don't really help recover the lost years, but I feel very sad that because of what I was told, someone like Mom and Dad were hurt so deeply.

Then I look at Mom and her incredible fortitude and character that helped her overcome the hurt and loss. I love touching her, holding her hand, hugging her. I love it when she says she loves me. But I feel so sad that she missed so much of my life. I shared pictures, report cards, Valentines, and letters from boyfriends; and she seemed to do well reviewing all of them. I was concerned she'd be hurt again, and I don't want to do anything to let her be hurt again.

She reads her Bible every morning; we said grace before dinner; she's an excellent cook; they liked the gifts I brought; Mom gave me her favorite opal and diamond ring! They are unselfish, generous, loving people; they're well traveled, have lots of friends, have worked hard as a team, and now enjoy retirement together very much.

How she isn't bitter and sad, I don't know. It's just amazing what she endured. Only the Lord in her life, and her own inner strength and determination to go on, could let her keep functioning in spite of her loss.

She loved Dad's daughter as her own, along with their daughter's friend, Carol. But even Dad said he's had 45 very difficult Mother's Days and

February birthdays. So, an underlying sadness must have persisted. It's hard to fathom how they survived the injustice.

How could father and my stepmother lie like they did and NEVER consider how they would have been hurt if it had happened to them??!!

We talked some about the past - but kept reminding each other we have to stay in the now and future. Dad mentioned a few times that he's glad I'm in her life in case anything would happen to him. He's worried for Mom's sake. It's amazing to me that he trusts me already to believe I'd be there for Mom if something happened to him. Of course, he's 100% correct, I'd be there for her without a doubt!

As soon as I saw Mom at the airport, I knew it was going to be a great weekend. She is a beautiful lady - outside and especially inside! She's a remarkable lady to handle all this and be such a cheerful, delightful person. She is a very capable businesswoman, but very content as Dad's wife.

They have a nice, comfortable place, with Teddy Bears everywhere! They re-arranged the guest room - or should I say the Teddy Bears' room, for me to stay in. I feel VERY WELCOME and well loved.

They seem to understand the "brainwashing and poison" I grew up with - and accept me now without reservation. I'm trying to go forward, but the lost years and the hurt they both endured, seem so unfair. I can't change the past, but will try to make the future better. They're part of my life now and I'm VERY GLAD for that! I guess, like my stepmother couldn't break my spirit (at least that's what close friends tell me), neither could adversity break Mom's. Incredible!

In the two weeks I've known Mom - and Dad - they have shown more interest in me than I've felt my father and stepmother had in decades! I know it's all new to Mom and Dad - but they do let me feel they really care and are interested.

Day 2 of the Reunion Weekend ...

Wow ... we had a very nice day!

Enjoyed talking with Mom this morning when she got up. She shared stories of her work that led to a lesson of going on with what we've got, and not looking back. In retail sales or banking jobs, she couldn't let her pain show. When you meet the public, you have to be able to smile, even when your heart is breaking like hers was. I couldn't hold back all the tears, but

Mom's hanging tough; she cried so many already, she says.

She told me real estate stories that made me laugh. At one Open House, she had to wear flea collars on her ankles because the fleas attacked her so badly! Another time, she was driving prospective buyers around the Clearwater area and was lost, but didn't want the buyers to lose confidence. So, she starts having them count the different kind of Florida palm trees, to see if they can guess how many kinds there are. She finally tells them the number is 32.

I asked, "Was that how many there are?"

She said, "I don't know, I just needed to buy time to find my way again!" The prospects did buy a house from her, by the way!

The Teddy Bear collection started with only one bear as a result of Mom breaking her neck in the early 1970's, when a train totaled her 1968 Cougar. A railroad crossing's view was blocked by high weeds and construction equipment and had no crossing guard. Mom inched up to see if a train was coming and there it was! She was thrown from the driver's seat into the back passenger seat by the crash impact. When she came to, she saw a man in a white coat looking into the car window, and thought he was greeting her at Heaven's gate. It was actually the steward from the caboose car coming to see if she was alive.

Long story short, they got her to the hospital and miraculously a famous surgeon for the President was in town and available to assist Mom! He was able to handle her case, which saved her life. She didn't have to have the halo drilled into her head, as I've seen used for a broken neck; but her neck had to be immobilized for several months. She couldn't move more than ¼" or ½" to the right or left. To help with that task, Dad bought her a little Teddy Bear and sat it by the pillow next to her head. If she could see the Bear to her right or in the mirror in front of her on the left, she was turning her head too much.

After a very long recovery period, her broken neck healed and she never even had headaches or arthritis in her neck! When I saw the picture of her totaled Cougar, it truly was a miracle I was sitting there talking with my Mom in person! Other than God's hand, there was no way she should have survived that train wreck.

To add insult to her injury, the police gave her a ticket for not yielding to the train! There is now an automated crossing guard at that railroad and street intersection! For obvious reasons, Mom preferred to use a different route after that incident!

Their friends, Bill and Chris, came over to visit in the afternoon, after we had spent the morning going over Mom and Dad's pictures. We shared with Chris and Bill the story of why it took 45 years to reunite; plus, we shared some of the birthday cake with them - not too much though, I was being selfish! It was too good to give away too generously!

Mom shared that she reunited with her mother and father several years after I had been taken from their house. I was incredulous that she had that much forgiveness in her heart. I asked why she would let them back into her life? She said she missed her father and felt sorry for the way her mother treated her father.

Eventually, her father and mother moved to Florida to be nearer to Mom and because they were tired of the cold Ohio winters. Mom said they never had a real close relationship, but a tolerable one.

She said Dad made sure her father and mother knew that Dad would not let them ever hurt Mom again. After that speech, both her father and mother treated Mom with more respect and knew they should never dare to incite the wrath of "the gentle giant!"

I also spoke with my godmother for the first time, someone I didn't even know I had in my life. Her name is "Aunt Norm" … Mom was named after her. She lived in Arizona, and hoped to be able to see me again some day. She was very happy I had reunited with Mom.

Mom shared with me that Aunt Norm was a little eccentric and would take some getting used to. Eccentric like wearing an old coat out to dinner, when she has a fine wardrobe, but doesn't want the wait staff to expect a big tip; or putting the extra sugar packets or extra rolls in her purse to take home when she has plenty of resources to afford them.

Mom does try to write to her weekly knowing she is a lonely widow and doesn't have many friends.

Mom told me she went to Arizona when Aunt Norm's husband died to help her, but didn't realize it would mean digging a hole in the hard, dry ground under the birdbath to bury the urn! That was more than Mom signed up for!

Besides that, Aunt Norm doesn't eat regularly, nor very much at meals. Mom was starving during her stay there. When Dad picked Mom up at the airport, she said she wanted to go to the nearest restaurant immediately. The waiter actually asked Dad where she had been that she was so hungry, based on all she ordered and ate!

My Aunt Phyl called to see how the reunion was going. I'm not too sure Mom was happy to hear from her. Mom and I spent some time discussing the letters from my stepmother and from me that Aunt Phyl claims to have and that Mom knew nothing about! The fact that her sister knew where I was and didn't let Mom know is not right. Mom now tolerates Aunt Phyl's calls, but just barely.

Mom told me the grade school mementos and other collectibles helped her to deal with the memories or questions of our missing years. As we went through them, however, I saw how much of my life she missed, like the long time in 1st and 2nd grade when I waited for my front teeth to come in and thought they never would; the 6th grade class displays from foreign countries, when I dressed like someone from some South American country; my first boyfriend in 7th grade; the final 8th grade report on countries that won the principal's special recognition; my high school graduation with honors and party afterwards; my company softball games and bowling tournaments; the sadness of lost loves; and the diagnoses and healing after several surgeries. Those were occasions she felt she should have been there for. But our situation robbed her of those motherly privileges.

Mom was up early on Sunday morning, crying when I got up. I asked if she was okay. She was going through the photos again, and said she was trying to comprehend all that she missed. So, I wasn't sure she wanted to keep the photos, souvenirs, and mementoes. But bravely she said if I didn't want them back, she wanted them. I said they were all hers, but encouraged her not to keep them or go through them if they would keep making her sad.

I had a similar reaction later in the weekend, when Mom and Dad were going through their photos with me, and I saw many of their special occasions of which I wasn't a part. It broke my heart too. More tears and journaling would be needed before acceptance would come. Mom and Dad offered for me to have any of their pictures also. So, I selected several of them for a scrapbook I planned to make, as soon as I could stop crying about the lost years.

Mom showed me a photo of our four generations. My Mom, me pouting because I didn't want to wear the dress they were making me wear, my Mom's mother (Grandma Banks), and my Mom's grandmother (my Great-

Grandmother Ruzicka). Mom told me my great-grandmother was a tough lady to get close to, not demonstrative at all; except I knew how to get around her. Mom said I'd go stand next to my great-grandmother, real close and quiet, until she'd acknowledge me. Then, she'd let me sit by her or on her lap. Everyone else was afraid of her, but not me.

Great-Grandma Ruzicka was actually a high Treasury official in the Czechoslovakian government during World War I, and was awarded the "Order of the White Lion" for her dedicated service. Mom let me have all of the old photos from World War I that showed my Great-Grandma with the government officials, and gave me the medal she received as a keepsake. Wow! I was impressed by this particular family history!

Cricket's dog-sitter called to say Cricket is doing well! That's a big relief! On a sad note for me, I learned that Mom is very allergic to dogs and cats. So, if she and Dad ever come to visit me, I'm not sure what I'll be able to do with Cricket. But I'll cross that bridge when we get to that point. No decisions on that this weekend.

A Georgia friend of Mom's called while I was near the telephone. Mom told me to answer the call. I said "Hello."

Mom's friend said, "Norma?"

I said, "No, this is her daughter. Would you like to talk with my mother?"

Margot replied, "Well! Yes, I believe I would!" Obviously, another lifetime friend who didn't know I existed! Mom had some explaining to do again … but I sensed she didn't mind doing it at this point.

Mom put a picture of me in her locket next to Dad's picture. It's a locket she always wears.

It seems like all we've been doing is eating. They eat three meals a day; I'm used to only eating two. So they don't understand why I eat so little. However, I have learned some interesting "dining rules" in this family already.

Mom said she doesn't have to eat the crust on sandwiches, like she used to when she was growing up; she said I don't have to either if I don't want to.

Also, if you want something different for dinner than the other diners are having, that is an acceptable option - anything goes that's in the refrigerator if you want to fix it. Amazing! Makes sense though - if you go to a restaurant, everyone doesn't eat the same food! But that isn't how I was raised, so it takes some getting used to.

If you want a bowl of cereal, you can have a combination of cereal choices, not just a bowl of one kind of cereal. Wow - what a novel idea!

And don't forget if there's a special dessert made, like a pineapple upside-down cake, you can have a slice even if it's before the company comes!

My Birthday Dinner Out ...

Speaking of dining, I'm told we are going out to Bern's Steakhouse in Tampa, the "best steakhouse in the world." I am still nervous and full from lunch, so I'm not very hungry; but will do my best because it means a lot to them.

Dad had bought me a beautiful orchid corsage, which I wore to dinner. He was really happy I liked it that much. I'm wearing it to church tomorrow too.

Dinner was impressive - but as I thought, I didn't eat too much. I was still too nervous. Leftovers will be great the next day though.

Dad made sure I received the grand tour of the kitchen and the wine cellar; Mom went along too. I don't think Dad felt too good. Maybe he's nervous too!

When we got home from Bern's, Mom had another gift for me to open, this time a birthday gift. It is a custom designed gold heart pendant, with another pink heart within it ... a "heart of my heart" she called it, as she says that's what I am to her. On the back is engraved "Mom 2-9-97," the first date of our reunion contact and our official reunion anniversary date going forward. Isn't she thoughtful! I just so happen to have a plain gold necklace with me, on which that gold heart pendant displays nicely. I wear it every day to this day!

We then watched a video of my "20-year Roast," given by my co-workers at my current employer. That way Mom and Dad got acquainted with many of my colleagues, especially some of those who helped make this reunion a reality.

That completed the update of my life and brought Mom current. I think she feels good about all we reviewed together.

Limited Childhood Memories ...

There are only two memories I have of my childhood time with Mom. I discussed both of them with her, because she asked what I remembered of my early years. I explained the rest were beaten out of me and I just can't recall more than these two. I know that made her sad, makes me very sad too. But I was being honest with her, as she asked me to be.

The one vague memory I had, I never knew where it came from. When we would go visit friends as I was growing up, I would ask if they had dolls lined up on a shelf at the top of their room somewhere. I could remember seeing dolls of different countries, but I didn't know where I'd seen them. No friends ever said they had been theirs.

But Mom said excitedly, "Oh Honey, those were in your bedroom when you were little! I had your father build a shelf near the top of your ceiling and displayed all of those collectible dolls from different countries!"

I said, "Isn't it interesting that father never admitted any knowledge of those dolls, when he heard me asking friends about them?!"

The second memory is that I used to spread out my arms as far as they would go and say to Mom, "I love you this much!" That memory pleased Mom very much. It is now a reality due to this special reunion! Today in my office, I have a Precious Moments statue of a little girl with her arms outspread, that is entitled, "I Love You This Much!" On my bed is a pillow of a round bunny rabbit, with short stubby arms and legs and long ears, with the stubby arms outstretched. The bunny is a gift from Mom. Imprinted on the bunny's belly are the words, "Janet, I love you this much! Mom."

Mom questioned further, "Don't you remember your rocking chair when you were a little girl?" But I didn't remember it at all. Mom told me I used to get sent to my room to sit in my rocking chair for "timeouts," when I needed to get my temper under control. She thought as hard as I rocked and as frequently as I was sent there, surely I wouldn't have forgotten that childhood recollection! Guess that distant, forgotten memory is subconsciously why my chair of choice today is a stuffed rocking chair!

Reflections on Reunion Day 2 ...

It's going to be very difficult for me to leave Mom on Monday, I can tell already! I told her at dinner that I already knew three things - and actually LOTS more - but only shared three at that time:

She's a beautiful lady, inside and out.

I'm very glad she's my Mom.

I love her.

She said she loves me too. It feels VERY GOOD to have Mom hug me and say she loves me. It's easy for me to respond to that love and share mine in return. On February 10, I was questioning if I could love her as my mother; by February 22, I was sure that was possible and could feel the love growing!

Dad is complimentary too, and seems to like me; I like him too. He says he can't believe how much like Mom I am, in mannerisms, voice, the way I say things and what I say, the way I've worked, as well as in the way we look alike.

I'm still enjoying the genuine laughs we've shared together too.

I don't feel as sad tonight about the past. Guess we're getting to the present and future.

Sometimes when I look at Mom, I really can't believe she's in my life for real! Mom and Dad are warm, friendly, loving people who I hope will stay in my life for a VERY LONG time!

Day 3 of Reunion Weekend ...

We had a lovely Sunday together.

After breakfast, we went to church. The pastor acknowledged us and prayed for us. We were welcomed and greeted by several with good wishes. My orchid looked nice, as did my new opal ring and "heart of my heart" necklace!

We went to the Cove Cay Country Club for lunch. Then, changed into comfortable clothes and took a drive in "Big Red" around Clearwater. Dad and Mom talked a lot about places we could visit and things we could see when I come to town. But I told them, I really just want to visit with them and get to know them better.

I got sad at times during the drive about the lost years, the years they were working in real estate together, the years Mom was in banking and Dad in sales for various companies. The years when they had hardships and illnesses; the times they had special celebrations, including Dad's surprise 50th birthday party, Mom's bank retirement celebration, and Mom's award banquet for real estate accomplishments; the get-togethers with close friends; the times they spent with Karyn and Carol; the trips they took. All times I had missed.

On the flip side, I know Mom missed the years of my growing up, my surgeries and illnesses, my friends, career moves, and travels; the good times and the bad ones. She's especially troubled about the 45-year separation, which would have been more tolerable for her, if life would have been good for me.

Sometimes I feel sorry for me ... most times, sorry for Mom. But she seems happy to go forward, and since we can't recover what's been lost, that appears the only choice.

I am so very glad I came on this trip. Mom said my sharing a lot of my history with her really helped her, especially the grade school years and the 20-year Roast. We talked lots of hours, and I feel I know them much better.

I learned Mom loves holidays! It shows in the table decoration displays, as well as throughout the condo, I'm told.

At Thanksgiving, Mom doesn't like for anyone to be alone on that day, which lends itself to having lots of new people at their house for dinner. One Thanksgiving, Dad got home from a business trip and started to open the front door when some man opened it for him. The man asked, "Who are you?"

Dad said, "I live here ... who are you?!"

The man said, "Norma invited me for Thanksgiving dinner so I didn't have to be by myself."

Dad said his usual, "Oh my!" and greeted Mom lovingly.

I feel loved, wanted, and welcome in their hearts and home. I like Mom's style, approach, example, and sense of humor. I love to see her marriage so happy with Dad and vice versa. They're a great couple!

We discussed whether Mom should go to Cleveland with me when I go see my Uncle Rich and Aunt Phyl. We decided "No." It could be too hurtful and I don't want her hurt anymore. It was more selfishness on my part to see Mom again soon if she went with me in mid-March, but there could be things said that would hurt her. Dad said she could come anytime to see me or to meet me somewhere. That's just like Dad to find a way to make Mom happy!

This has been one birthday I'll NEVER forget ... and NEVER regret!

While there are some things still on my mind and heart, I know without a doubt that my Mom loves me, cares for me, and ALWAYS has. I can learn from her, enjoy being with her, and will miss her greatly when I leave tomorrow.

Heading Home on Day 4 ...

Mom and Dad won't hear of me taking a taxi to the airport to save them the driving. I'm just as glad, because I get to spend more time with them. I sit in the back, with my hand over the front seat resting on Mom's shoulder. I still need the feel of touching her for as long as I can. I watch out the window looking at Tampa Bay, hoping to see dolphins, but none today!

Now I sit between them in the Terminal waiting for the flight to be called. I can't believe it's time to go home already.

I know I must plan the next trip soon, so I won't miss Mom so much. Even though we call each other twice a day, morning and night, it's not the same as being with her in person, holding her hand, getting a hug when I want one - or getting spoiled in-person by my mother's unconditional love!

We part with the promise of calling as soon as I get home and keeping in touch frequently.

The flight attendants asked about my corsage, which gave me the opportunity to tell them Mom's and my reunion story. They cried. One asked me for information on locating her son's Dad. Isn't it great how the Lord is using our pain for someone else's gain already?!

I called Mom from the Denver stopover, to thank them for the delightful stay.

Checking In at Home and Work ...

I arrive home to be welcomed by my "kid," Cricket. She seems to be feeling better on the new medicines. That's a relief!

I start unpacking ... and find little "love notes" in my suitcase from Mom! She says she loves me and that I should never forget that! It's funny because I too left some notes for them in various parts of their condo! More signs that we think alike!

I also have mail from Mom and Dad waiting for me ... a loving birthday card ... and a special card with a dog on the front that looks like Cricket, but the dog's looking down at the ground. Inside the verse says, "I feel down when you're not around."

The greeting says "Hi Sweetheart" ... and I can hear her say it now. She tells me the dog looks a little like Cricket. She says they are looking forward to my next visit and have to start planning for it. She adds that she wanted me to have mail to come home to. She signs it, "We love you, Mom and Dad."

Lots of friends left voice messages at home and sent emails to see how the reunion went. It's such a relief to have them supportive and encouraging about my efforts, rather than critical or questioning about what I'm doing. I've had enough questions of my own! But seem to be on the right track; with God's help we'll keep going in the right direction.

Then, when I returned to work later that day, I saw the beautiful birthday flowers and balloons from Mom and Dad.

People welcomed me back to work and wanted an update on the successful reunion.

I already decided on the way home that I need to see Mom and Dad as soon as possible again - didn't get enough of their love and company. I'll change my Cleveland trip to stopover in Tampa and spend the weekend with Mom and Dad, rather than the Ohio relatives.

Plans in Process in Clearwater ...

When I call Mom to tell her of my change in travel plans for March, she had a big surprise for me!

She is already in the process of giving away most of her Teddy bears from the spare room. She wants to free up the spare bedroom for when I come to visit. The bears are being given to retirement centers and hospitals.

"You don't have to do that," I say quickly. "I can just push the bears to the side and work around them while I'm there."

"No Honey, you don't understand," she responds lovingly. "I don't need them anymore ... I have you now!"

Mom said as they drove away from one retirement center where they donated the huge white Teddy Bears, they saw residents already hugging and loving them. So, Mom knew it was the right decision and they went to a good home.

Another special reunion moment I'll never forget!

Mom says she is getting ready to start the scrapbook from the mementoes I left with her.

She also suggested I bring clothes that I can just leave at the condo, rather than always take some back and forth. Very thoughtful!

She told me she's proud of me and only wants the best for me. She worries that I'm not eating enough, nor getting enough rest. I told her it's nice to have someone worry about me. It's also nice to have someone love me like she does. She says likewise.

Reflections About the Reunion Weekend ...

After being surrounded by so many bears this weekend and hearing Mom say that she will do her best to see that I never get hurt again, I feel like I'm loved by "Mama and Papa Bear!"

We both agreed that while there is a lot of happiness from our reunion, there has been plenty of pain and tears as well. We believe that most of those reunion stories featured on TV don't last long because of the pain involved. The parties probably meet for a brief or one-time reunion; then, get on separate planes and head off into the sunset for safe zones again. You have to be willing to work through the hurt and losses in order to gain the ground needed to build on a long-term relationship. I realize these past two weeks are only a start, and we have much more pain and history to keep working through. Without the Lord in Mom's and my lives and His helping us with this reunion process, I know it wouldn't be possible.

It hasn't taken very long for me to become Mom's spoiled "kid!" While we are adult-to-adult in our new relationship, there is already a feeling that I am her "kid" and always will be.

I know one thing for sure after this reunion trip: she will ALWAYS be my loving Mom!

*   *   *   *   *

We've made good progress in our relationship with this successful and unforgettable reunion weekend.

But we're not off that "wild roller coaster ride" yet!

Chapter 4

A BI-COASTAL ROLLER COASTER

"I will lift up mine eyes unto the hills,
From whence cometh my help.
The Lord shall preserve thy going out and thy coming in
from this time forth, and even for evermore."
Psalm 121:1 and 8

Flying back to California from the Clearwater reunion weekend, I was on an all-time high!

It was wonderful to finally meet Mom, to understand what a special lady she was, and to know she would be my mother forever. Meeting Dad was a plus too, as he was a very thoughtful, caring person, and now my step-dad. They were now my family.

But visiting with them four days was just not enough! You can't cram 45 missing years into four days and feel like you know these two people; you can't be sure you love them; and you can't understand what made them who they are - all in such a short timeframe. Come to find out, they felt the same about me.

So, we found ourselves trying to settle down to a bi-coastal living arrangement.

Ways We Kept in Touch ...
Calling twice each day, gave me a $700 phone bill the first month! But it

was important to keep getting to know one another gradually. Besides hearing Mom's voice so happy to hear from me always gave me a lift!

After the first month, Dad asked, "What do you two have to talk about so much?"

Mom said, "About 45 years worth!" That ended that discussion.

It wouldn't always be me initiating the calls. Mom would call me too before or after work, to help share the phone bill costs. Sometimes our talks were brief; other times, lots to say.

She was still taking notes on likes and dislikes. Mom had the wisdom of age, and the advantage of our adult-to-adult relationship, to recognize "hot buttons" or things that I felt strongly about, and was careful and thoughtful not to be judgmental or too opinionated at the wrong moments.

Other times, she was very encouraging or tactful to provide insight I needed into decisions or life in general. She was a very intelligent lady and my mother, and I respected both of those roles she now played in my life.

We also kept the greeting card companies' stock going up with almost daily communications. I even received birthday and Christmas cards from owners of the card stores I most often frequented; that's when you know you shop there a lot!

Cards and calls were exchanged on the 9th of each month to commemorate our special reunion anniversary date.

The local florist was delighted with our reunion going well. We got to be personal friends through the subsequent orders - those Mom would send to me in California and those that I'd order from that florist to send to Mom and Dad in Clearwater.

We were very caring, but not seeing one another enough to either's satisfaction.

California to Clearwater Commuting ...

My product planning and agency relations work assignments required some cross-country travel that allowed me to add periodic stopovers in Clearwater at no additional costs to my employer; but scheduling those trips would not be on a regular basis.

When one business trip would end in the current week, and another planned to start sometime the following week, I would book a "red-eye" connecting flight between the trips. This would allow me to travel into

Tampa/Clearwater for a weekend stay that would allow me a 2- or 3-day visit with Mom and Dad.

We would look forward to a scheduled visit or trip. We'd do a countdown of the days until I'd fly into Tampa. They'd meet my flight. Then, we'd think, half way through the visit, that the visit was just too short. All too soon, I'd be back on a plane returning home ... not knowing when the next visit could occur. Even if the next trip was a ways off, knowing there was another one scheduled gave great comfort for all of us.

I tried to commute on special occasions using vacation and holidays tied into weekends for some quick visits.

Whenever a visit was being scheduled, Mom and Dad assured me they always welcomed it. I finally stopped asking if they had anything planned on certain dates that I was thinking of visiting them, because they always cleared their calendar to accommodate my schedule. Dad would tell people, "The kid's coming to town this weekend," which folks knew meant I came first in plans for that timeframe. It was cute to be considered their "kid" at 50 years old!

When a visit included a Sunday, we always attended church together. If I'd get into town on Thursday or early on Friday, I joined Mom and Dad for Bingo at the Village Clubhouse on Friday nights.

When I'd arrive on a "red-eye," Mom and Dad would wait up for me. I'd eat the refreshments Mom had prepared. Then, I'd get to bed late and sleep late the next day. But I didn't sleep too much because I came all that way to visit with them.

This type of schedule, the stress of travel, and trying to keep up with work assignments, would take its toll on me eventually. It was a very important investment for me, however, to be with them whenever I could. I had been given a special opportunity from the Lord. I didn't know how many days ahead I would have them in my life and I didn't want to waste even a day of it.

When I look back at my 1997 calendar, I actually visited Clearwater 1 to 3 times per month, primarily on a weekend. That year, I made 19 trips to Clearwater, for a total of 75 days. The trips originated from various points in the country, depending on whether the trip was vacation or business related. But each trip left us wishing we were closer in proximity.

Mom wrote, "I wish you lived next door to us for the rest of our lives." It was a strong tug at my heart to hear this from Mom. I knew it wasn't practical, or financially feasible, at this time. But I certainly did pray about it and do the math!

I did want to know them better; to be there to help them when and where I could; to be part of their life for as long as I had been given the privilege. They felt the same as I did. Without wanting to crowd me, they were interested in my life, willing to be there and assist when needed, or just love me if that's what I needed most. They even talked about finding a way to allow me to be a nearby neighbor, when a condo unit in their building became available. But that wasn't the Lord's plan for now, and I was trying to listen and obey whatever God had planned for going forward.

So, commuting when I could was the best option at the time. The airlines were thrilled with the business, I'm sure, and tickets using frequent flier mileage helped hold down some costs.

I was often able to work remotely based on certain job assignments. I'd sit on Mom and Dad's patio doing my stack of work. They were content to just have me nearby. Dad said, "One thing for sure, Ed (my father) had to raise a "little Norma" all those years!" (which Dad felt father deserved for what he did to Mom.) Dad commented on how much alike Mom and I were and said, "Seeing Janet is like watching Norma in a mirror."

Mom and Dad understood that my job demanded the extra hours. They also had those kinds of jobs. I was fortunate to have a self-sufficient, supportive team at the office, operating independently while I was traveling. Thanks to conference calls, voice messaging, and emails, we were able to keep business progress happening as needed.

We planned our family get-togethers to be "visiting intense." We spent much of the time talking and learning about each other and sharing our lives before we reunited. We would even eat most meals in, to allow more time to visit, rather than taking time to drive to restaurants, wait for tables, then have to drive home. Because Mom was a terrific cook and loved to do it, she would spend much of the week before I arrived preparing meals for us to partake. She actually received great joy from our plans to eat at home. My appetite improved as we got better acquainted and my nervousness subsided. I'm not sure my weight gain was a delight to my doctor, but Mom felt good about it!

We enjoyed several 1997 holidays and special occasions together including Mother's Day, Father's Day, Mom's and Dad's birthdays, Thanksgiving, Christmas, and New Years.

Life at Cove Cay ...

I didn't want Mom and Dad to keep trying to pick me up at the airport due to many late night arrivals. So, we negotiated that I would use the taxi service and they could stay up and wait for me if they insisted. We compromised on this arrival strategy.

Mom prepared a schedule of her activities at my request for me to be able to call her daily. Between her pool exercise class, doctor visits, errands, Club lunches, Bingo games, and other activities, she was a very active senior citizen. Add to that the 3-hour time difference between us, and I had trouble figuring out where she was when! She happily provided the schedule to allow our daily communications to continue.

It didn't take too many visits before Mom and Dad insisted they were going to remodel the spare room and make it more my bedroom and office. So, they asked me to select furniture I wanted and make it a second home for myself.

Just so I wouldn't forget what my "second home" looked like, Mom found lots of pictures of Cove Cay to send me for reference. It is a lovely location bordering Tampa Bay, with the golf course intertwined among the condo buildings.

One day, I started out the front door to bring in their mail only to be met by a large black snake trying to climb the wall! I quietly closed the door and calmly inquired, "Does anyone care that there's a snake out front?!"

Mom suggested I get the maintenance man to catch the snake and dispose of it, which meant I had to go back outside! Anyway, Hector got it with a rake and tossed it into the pond nearby ... to come visit us another day, I guess! I was hoping for its head to get chopped off!

My friend Diane talked with me about considering taking some of my clothes with me on the next trip and leaving them at Mom's. Diane said that sent an important healing message that I was coming back, as well as feeling comfortable as part of the family. Actually, I was still working on that last thought! I felt like a guest, not yet family. It wasn't their fault. It was just taking me time to adjust to their love and hospitality. Visiting was joyful, yet still scary for me. What if they didn't like me and rejected me? There was risk from my perspective that our relationship was still tentative.

During my March trip preparations, I did pack ½ of a suitcase with clothes I would leave there. Boy, did that make them happy! My friend was absolutely correct!

In March, I met Carol, who was like my Mom and Dad's daughter in my absence. She was such a good friend, caring about Mom and Dad so much that she had offered them to stay in a wing of her house if anything happened that they required in-home care. I can still recall her leaving that first day we met saying, "You may not have had any sisters, but now you have one in Florida!" She truly has been a good friend in the years since we met. Frequently, Carol would be included in plans during my Clearwater visits to Mom and Dad's.

Lots of Ups and Downs ...

After the reunion weekend, both Mom and I felt good about the weekend ... but hurts would surface periodically, when I'd least expect it, usually when I was tired, I was most vulnerable. While lots of things were going well, I would suddenly get sad about the lost years, about special times in Mom's and Dad's lives that I missed, about love and encouragement from a mother that would never be mine due to our years apart.

I kept journaling my thoughts and feelings. When they would still overwhelm, I would book an appointment with Beverly to help sort them out and straighten out my priorities.

Mom would start working on the scrapbook only to suddenly feel it was too painful. She would pick up the materials to start its assembly, only to be slammed by sadness, regrets, and then anger about what she missed in my life. Dad encouraged her to tell me about it; he said, "She's a grown woman, she'll understand."

Finally, during my March visit with them, Mom admitted to me it was too hard to do the scrapbook and asked that I take back the school pictures and Valentines. I understood and was willing to do that. I sure didn't want to bring her any more sadness than life had already caused her.

People, who don't know what it's like to lose someone you love for 45 years, might not understand how we couldn't get past these types of hurdles. But it takes time to work through and overcome them. It took much prayer. It took counseling when I would get overwhelmed. It took trying to forgive and forget only to realize these are beyond human capabilities at times, and we were only human.

Mom later confided that Dad and she thought I was very brave to visit them during the reunion weekend, when a lot of reunions don't end happily. I never entertained that was a possibility. After God told me He'd help me to love Mom through His eyes, I knew it would be done. I just needed time and frequency of interfacing to allow the love to grow. Mom was easy to talk to on the phone, and my days weren't complete unless I did. However, infrequent visits didn't allow that day-to-day growing love to happen as quickly as I thought it would. Trust builds gradually; love does too, I learned.

On the front of one card Mom sent me, a bear is standing in his pajamas wearing a sleep hat. Imprinted on the front of the card it says, "Somebody has been sleeping in my bed" … and Mom added, "and it is my favorite daughter!"

In another card, the front showed a baby in a diaper with a snorkel facemask on her head and flippers on her feet. The card says, "I've flipped over you!" Mom wrote, "Because you are my kid … and, if I had mailed God an order, it would be to your 'specs.' Love you, Baby!"

Our hairdressers on both Coasts were shaking their heads.

My West Coast hairdresser of several decades, Sharon, was shocked when I told her I was reuniting with my birth mother. Sharon said, "I knew there was something different between your hair and hers (my stepmother's)! Now I understand why your heads of hair were totally different!"

On the East Coast, Mom's hairdresser, Marie, had been doing her hair for over 20 years. Surprisingly, Marie was one of those, like Mom's many friends in Clearwater, who didn't know I even existed! When Mom asked Marie to fix her hair up nicely for our reunion visit, Marie was shocked to learn about me.

After the reunion, Marie asked Mom about the experience of seeing me at the airport. Mom said, "I knew her right away - it was like looking in a mirror!"

Marie now does my hair too, and says I "have my mother's hair, you poor thing!"

In one phone conversation, I told Mom I had some bronzed baby shoe bookends. She seemed genuinely pleased that I still had them. I actually didn't know they were MY baby shoes! She told me her father had them bronzed at a time money was very scarce. They meant more with the history behind them. Before I located Mom, I had told my sister-in-law about the bookends and offered them to her. But she wouldn't take them, commenting, "That's a keepsake for you." When Mom found out I had them, I asked her if she'd like them and she was thrilled with the offer. She kept one in her kitchen, to hold up the cookbooks, the other in the headboard of her bed, holding up paperbacks. She was pleased to have that memory of my past nearby.

I grew up not caring for my middle name, Gayle. I don't know why I objected, maybe it's just a thing kids do. But when I found out Mom picked out both my names, they became special to me. She also had given me a nickname, combining Janet and Gayle into J'Gay. I liked it, so she called me that. Except when she was upset with me on rare occasions, then it was "Janet Gayle!" She tried to call me "Jan," which was the name I used in business for several decades. But it never sounded right when she used it, so I asked her to call me Janet or J'Gay. She was happy to comply!

I notified Aunt Phyl and Uncle Rich that I would not be coming to Ohio in March as planned. Getting to know Mom and Dad in Clearwater and timing those trips around my work responsibilities required postponing a reunion with more relatives for a while. I honestly felt I couldn't handle more emotional situations after just meeting Mom and Dad. I really needed to solidify our relationship first.

Coupled with a business trip, I did visit Reno to see my half-brother and family. I wanted to keep them informed of the reunion's success and on-going new family relationship. These topics weren't met with great enthusiasm by my half-brother; but my sister-in-law was happy for me.

> In a card from Mom between my visits, she wrote, "It still doesn't seem possible that you are back in my life again … I used to think I could walk past you and not know you were mine - but now I'm not so certain of that (especially the quivering chin.) My baby - I love you so much you will never know. There aren't enough words to tell you."

My boss advised me to not make any serious decisions about relocating for at least a year. But it was tempting. When I'd travel to the various locations, I'd consider if working closer to Mom and Dad's proximity would be advantageous. Later, my boss offered if I decided I needed to relocate closer to them, he'd be supportive of that. It was a helpful offer, even though I never used it.

My life was filled with various financial challenges around the time of our reunion. The extra travel expenses incurred added to those issues. Mom and

Dad proved to be trustworthy experienced guidance counselors to help me plan solutions to those problems. In some cases they even offered financial assistance, which I generally declined, as that wasn't why I wanted them in my life. I just appreciated their unbiased approach and recommended alternatives.

In a card to Mom after returning home, I wrote, "Sorry for my periods of introspection that may have clouded my visit. As usual, it's not either of you that are troubling me. It's the things I missed and those in my past who took from me, that I'm having to face. The many life changes I've had are not as easy for me to cope with as I thought. Even more, playing my daily role requires greater fortitude than I realized would be needed at this point. But your love and encouragement are very welcome and appreciated. Your prayers and counsel help my coping and determination."

Someone Else Blessed Along the Way ...

Several years ago, my friend, Sally, introduced me to a friend of hers named Lauren Stratford. Lauren had been the victim of severe child abuse and several other tragic abuses in her life, which she documented in books entitled, "Satan's Underground" and "I Know You're Hurting." Sally loaned me those books while I was recuperating from foot surgery a few years before my whole recovery process began unfolding. God used those books to plant a seed for me to eventually face my abuse.

When I went into therapy, Lauren was an "encourager" through the pain of the healing process. When I found my birth mother, Lauren was a "cheerleader" through the reunion and subsequent visits. Lauren was happy for me to find healing and be able to establish a good relationship with my mother, whereas Lauren's story didn't end as happily.

Lauren wrote me a card after the reunion that said,

"I just glow when I hear all the wonderful things (miracles) God is doing in your life. Oh how much He loves you! You were in 'God's Waiting Room' for so long. You've learned so much that will help and encourage others in their waiting rooms. You are God's living example of HOPE! What a proof positive you are that God does work all things out in His time."

Because my story meant so much to Lauren, someone who had been hurt beyond belief, I kept in touch with her, sharing the joys and learning experiences of my new life. Until the Lord rescued Lauren from her pain and took her home to Heaven, Lauren's heart was uplifted each time she heard about Mom's and my growing love for each other. The "family" experience I was able to enjoy was something Lauren could only dream about. Living it along with me gave her comfort and joy.

Lauren wrote a note to my Mom in March 1997:

> Dear Norma,
>
> Jan has been a gracious friend of mine for several years. I asked her if I could write a thank you note to you for opening your heart and arms to her.
>
> When Jan flew to meet you for the first time, I think I held my breath until I next heard from her. I was fearing the worst, but hoping for the best. When she called me after the reunion, I needed only to hear the sound of her voice, and I knew without a doubt that she had found the very best! I've never seen such a dramatic change in one person's life.
>
> God has graced you and your daughter with many years to share such a beautiful love. I pray that through this love, Peace and Joy will begin to heal the years of loss and pain.
>
> You have a wonderful daughter, and in listening to Jan, I know she has a wonderful Mom. I cannot express just how much this miracle reunion has touched my own life.
>
> Thank you and God bless.
> Lauren Stratford

An Easter Message I Never Fully Understood Before …

I wrote an Easter message for Mom and Dad, because some things were easier to say in writing than in person. When they received it, Dad said he almost cried, Mom said she did. Mom said it really meant a lot to her:

"UNCONDITIONALLY" LOVED!

> At Easter time, it seems like we have some of the greatest illustrations of unconditional love in the crucifixion story. Even in the midst of their agony, Christ forgave the thief when asked. Christ then forgave all who were part of His torment and unjust punishment with

"Father forgive them for they know not what they do."

But for this Easter season, my greatest illustration of unconditional love is what has been occurring in my life since February 9, 1997. That was the day that my mother and I spoke for the first time in 45 years. God's conviction in my life was to find her to ask her forgiveness for having judged her all those years, when only the Lord has the right to judge. When Mom answered my call, and I told her who I was, my mother lovingly replied; "Hi Sweetheart, how are you?" As if no time had passed between our last conversation, just like she had hoped for my call every day of those 45 years. I was instantly forgiven for any part I had in our lack of contact. Love unconditionally that only a mother can give to her child. I had never experienced that kind of love. No matter what I do or have done, she still loves me. It's an amazing picture of God's love too. My heart was flooded, and still is, with "joy unspeakable", realizing that a person on earth can love me as God does ... unconditionally. I feel so blessed.

So this Easter, I understand better than ever what God's gift of His Son means to us. He loves us the same way my mother, Norma Wallace, loves me ... unconditionally. And only God, who loved us so unconditionally that He gave His only Son so we might have the gifts of eternal life and love, could create a mother's heart with such a precious gift of unconditional love for her children.

Thank you, Mom, for the special gift of love you have given to me this year, and forever ... because of the Easter story.

With love, Jan
Your daughter
3/30/97

Mom and Dad's pastor asked for permission in April to reprint this Easter message in their monthly church newsletter. He believed it would help his congregation think beyond their boundaries. That pleased Mom very much.

A Note to Mom in April ...

Good Morning, Mom!

How's my favorite person in the whole world? Hope you had a

good night's rest. Thanks for the delicious dinner, your usual special hospitality, and the good conversation we had. I feel very welcome here. I feel loved like I've never been before.

I enjoyed finding your note in my bedding! You are so **special** to me, and **such** a **thoughtful** person. I'm still not sure **why** all this has happened - but I do know that I've laughed more, been loved more, and grown more in the past 2 ½ months, than I have for decades.

Thanks for being part of this miracle we are living. If I could have picked a mother - she would have been you. Thanks for all you are and mean to me already.

Love you back,
Jan

Our relationship was growing more special with each passing day.

A card Mom wrote to me in April included these special words, "If God had paraded 1,000+ daughters in front of me, my choice would have been you in a heartbeat! We have a lot of 'getting to know you' time ahead of us, but feel closer to you daily. I hope you feel the same way."

She closed another card in May with, "You are 1 sweet kid and all mine!! Your Mom"

More Ups and Downs on our Wild Ride ...

Mom mentioned we're doing well getting to know each other. But she told some friends, "It's not as easy as you think to get acquainted. Janet's 50 years old and I don't even know if she likes peanut butter!"

Then she looked at me and said, "I don't even know what your favorite meal is!"

I said, "I'm not sure I know - no one's ever asked me before. I'm used to pleasing everyone else!"

I gave Mom a dessert recipe during my March visit. I mentioned that recipe to her as I prepared for the April trip. What do you think she had waiting for me when I next visited? Yep! She made that dessert just for me for the April visit. Yum! She felt if it was that important for me to mention it again, she didn't want to disappoint me. Isn't she something!

Mom told me she felt she doesn't witness effectively. But she mentioned a comment by a former pastor that I told her shows she certainly does have an effective witness by her actions. The pastor commented how everyone notices she and Dad hold hands in the second row of church and added what an inspiration their love for each other and the Lord are to others. I told her folks who've known her to be the happy, special person she's been all these years, had to be impressed that she lived that way in spite of the 45 years of deep hurting. That's a pretty impressive witness from my perspective.

In the same conversation, I told Mom that I don't believe God's done using our reunion story yet either. He didn't bring us together to cause us more pain; but He does want us to be witnesses for Him by using our story in ways that have yet to be revealed.

Maybe our story will help someone like the IRS person I spoke with shortly before this conversation. The IRS person was considering whether she should look up her birth father after many years. I told her to "remember there are two sides to every story!" She was going to explore that possibility!

I met Mom and Dad's godson, Andrew, during my April visit. What a nice young man he was, so handsome and personable. When he left, he hugged me and said, "We're almost like brother and sister now." Everyone I met makes me feel more like family.

Bad headaches were frequently occurring during the time of my commuting to see Mom and Dad. Traveling cross-country at odd hours, working on numerous work priorities, and handling financial stresses were undoubtedly root causes of many of those headaches. Add to that the anxiety of developing the new family relationships. Altogether these issues made for some emotional times for me.

During my April visit, the past came back to haunt me once again. I couldn't get my tears under control from being upset with father. I thought "how could someone be so mean to keep their child from her mother? How could a father let his daughter think her whole life that she wasn't wanted and wasn't loved by her mother? How could a man punish a woman, like father did Mom, and deprive her of so many events in her child's life?"

My head told me we couldn't make up for what was lost; but my heart had trouble accepting the hurts Mom and I endured because of father's decisions. I'm not sure if it was father's selfish love or his need to punish Mom that led him to his hurtful actions. Whatever the cause, it was still bothering me.

I shared some of these feelings in a lengthy note to Mom written one night during this April visit. In my note, I told Mom she was the only one I could really share these feelings with who could understand. But I didn't want to hurt her further in the process.

The next day, she said she knows it's hard, but we just had to go on. She admitted that some hurts still bothered her a lot too. She didn't understand how a stepmother "steps on the child," instead of "stepping in for the parent" like she did for Bill's daughter. And she added she sure didn't understand why father allowed me to be treated the way he did.

It took lots of tears for me to pull out of this setback. Mom cried too while trying to comfort me.

Fortunately, these setbacks were getting less frequent. Laughter and good conversation were more prevalent in our times together. More stories from Mom and Dad filled in the background of their lives together, so I could better understand the kinds of people they were. New memories were replacing the hurts of the past.

Work was taking a secondary priority. Actually, I wasn't enjoying work like I used to. I was working hard remotely, trying to keep up with job expectations. I knew I needed the job and benefits and it was too early to retire. The ability to travel was very generous, allowing me to get to know Mom and Dad on stopovers between business trips. Some day I might try relocating closer to Mom and Dad, so that was another reason to keep doing a good job for my employer. So, it was time for me to have a positive attitude adjustment. A vacation away from everything might be very helpful; maybe the Greek Cruise planned for May was the answer.

But before that, a memorable event was about to take place.

First Mother's Day Together in 45 Years! …

We were able to celebrate Mother's Day together in California, thanks to Mom and Dad's previously planned West Coast vacation trip. Dad and I had spoken about it for over two months. I wanted to know where they would be on Mother's Day in their vacation plans, so I could surprise Mom with some kind of Mother's Day recognition. But Dad was determined to make our physically being together that day a reality!

It is a very long journey from Florida to California at any age; but at 73, it was even more demanding on Dad with his intention in mind. He

STOLEN BUT NOT LOST

pressed that gas pedal steadily from coast to coast, ensuring their journey would end timely in California to allow us to be together on that special day, our first Mother's Day in 45 years! Mom was actually oblivious to what Dad was trying to do. Remember, Mother's Day was a day for her to forget normally - but not this one!

Mom and Dad traveled with two of their Cove Cay friends, Chris and Bill, making nightly stops in various cities between Clearwater and Southern California. They were actually on their way to Seattle, Washington to see the Space Needle as their ultimate destination before returning to Florida via a more Northwestern route.

I recently learned that Mom wasn't actually interested in going by way of California in their Seattle quest because of the California earthquakes! But that theory went out the window when I showed up on the scene. All of a sudden, Covina, California was a definite destination for their cross-country vacation plans! Seattle became a secondary goal.

Of course, I was delighted they were coming my way, and started making plans for this special event in our lives:

- I made them reservations at a nearby hotel, due to limited sleeping space at my house and considering Mom's allergy to Cricket.
- We had Sunday reservations at a lovely restaurant for Mother's Day brunch. Our reunion story got us a nice table reserved for our party.
- A Saturday reception at my house was planned, inviting new and old friends and neighbors to meet Mom.

When Mom and Dad and their friends arrived at my house, we were able to sit in the backyard and visit a bit. Mom got to meet Cricket for the first time. That wasn't instant love either. Cricket is a Chow, a breed that tends to favor one-person, I was told. My "spoiled brat" certainly fit that description! So, Mom would have an uphill battle winning over Cricket, a battle she eventually undertook, by the way, with good results!

I soon learned it was just as well that Mom couldn't go into the house for very long, because Dad confided in me how difficult it was for Mom to face the house. She viewed it as my father's and stepmother's house, the house where I had been raised and abused. I hadn't given that a thought, as I was so happy for us to be together for this special Mother's Day weekend! So, I spoke with Mom about how I viewed this as MY house; I had maintained it, kept it updated, bought almost everything in it, and had inherited it from father and my stepmother's estate. So, I didn't view it as father's and my stepmother's house. I asked if she could try to see it from my viewpoint. Of course she tried. I knew it was still painful for her, but I didn't really have a choice; it was my home, the only one I could afford at the time.

The "Meet My Mom" Event ...

The meet and greet event was named, "Welcome to Teddy Bears' Picnic and Meet My Mom." It was staged in my backyard, due to Mom's allergy to Cricket.

After planning this event and sending out the invitations, it dawned on me that Mom was also very allergic to the Bottle Brush trees in my backyard. So, I had to hire the gardener to quickly dispose of them.

I arranged for catered food. Neighbors donated tables and chairs to the cause. Everyone I invited arranged, on short notice, to attend. I was thrilled ... and nervous, but probably not half as nervous as Mom was to meet everyone for the first time.

Naturally, Mom was the center of attention as the guests arrived. As Dad had told me, anyone who met Mom liked her ... and this was no exception. Everyone enjoyed visiting and eating. No one was in a hurry to leave. It took a while for Mom to be able to visit with the various friends and family who attended.

A few special memories were created at the reception:

I had an album of old family, black and white pictures, none of which had identifying names on them. I didn't recognize whose pictures they were, and consequently wasn't interested in keeping them. Since many old family friends were in attendance, I offered the photos to them if they recognized anyone in the pictures. As people were visiting with Mom and turning the album pages, all of a sudden a bald, naked baby picture appeared and Mom surprisingly said, "Janet, here's your baby picture!"

"You've got to be kidding!" I said.

Mom replied, "No, it's you!" She sounded delighted to recognize me! Then, added, "Your Grandmother told me, 'Someday Janet will not be happy that you took this photo of her!'"

"Well, I guess that day has arrived," I commented, "and in front of all my friends! How memorable!" At that point, I removed the photo and presented it to Mom as a keepsake! We all had a good laugh.

Later, I was trying to get Mom's attention, while speaking to her from a different part of the yard. I said, "Mom," while looking at my Mom. No answer, except a few 'Moms' nearby looked up.

So, I said a little louder, "Mom!" Now all the 'mothers' were looking at me, giving their full attention - but not my mother. She continued to converse with others around her.

Finally, I said loudly, "Norma!" She looked up right away. Everyone started laughing.

I said, "Mom, one thing's for sure, you have to learn your new name! I've been calling 'Mom' and you're the only one who doesn't acknowledge the name yet!"

Then I went over and hugged her. Everyone laughed and applauded.

There was one shocking moment that day. One of the guests, on my stepmother's side, said to Mom, "I thought you were dead!"

"Apparently not!" Mom responded quite offended.

The guest said, "That's what I was told about why you weren't in Janet's life. No one ever corrected that story."

They discussed the situation a little more to clarify what the guest had been told and possible reasons why. But here was some additional fallout from the lies perpetuated by my father and stepmother. Some family and friends knew the truth; others were told stories like this one, that my mother was dead.

It was hurtful for Mom that day when this was said, but she pressed on somehow. I can only imagine what was going through Mom's mind while she was trying to be cordial to guests.

My counselor, Beverly, was one of the first people I invited to this special "Meet My Mom" get-together. Beverly's counsel had made this reunion possible, so there was no way I wanted her to miss meeting Mom in-person. It was mutual on Beverly's part; and Mom was happy to meet and thank Beverly for her role in our reunion.

Recently, I learned that Mom took Beverly aside that day and spoke with her about our new relationship. Mom's comment to Beverly, with tears in her eyes, was that she "just had to be able to spend more time with me and didn't know how she would be able to do it with the distance between us." Apparently, Mom was feeling like I was, that our brief chats and visits were not satisfying enough. Beverly's counsel to Mom that day was to "just give it time and take it one day at a time." Mom never mentioned that discussion to me; she just endured our trying to get to know one another better whenever time and schedules permitted. What a strong lady my Mom was!

Everyone seemed to have a good time visiting with Mom and getting to know her a little. She was a hit as predicted and I was very proud of her!

Special Mother's Day Brunch …

Mom got to see "her kid in action" during the special Mother's Day Brunch. I had arranged for special restaurant seating with the manager. Seating was to be in the dining room part of the restaurant, in cushy, high Queen-backed chairs. Special waiters were to be assigned to our table. While it was a serve-yourself brunch, seating in this restaurant room was to assure us extra special service.

However, when we arrived, the host took us into a huge banquet room filled with hundreds of other seats at large round tables. You could hardly maneuver around the tables. On top of that, our tablecloth had holes in it! I kidded and said, "If you put the salt shaker over that hole, and the pepper shaker on the other side of the table over that hole, maybe no one will notice!" All the time I was fuming! This was to be a very special and memorable occasion! It was turning memorable all right - but for the wrong reasons!!

As our party proceeded to the buffet food for the first course, I "bee-lined" out to the manager's podium, where I explained that this was not the seating I ordered, nor was I impressed with holes in our tablecloth. I demanded our seating be changed to what I had pre-arranged. She knew I was upset; she listened as I explained why this was so important to me; and proceeded to rectify the situation.

Meanwhile, Dad asked Mom, "Where is Janet going?"

She said, "I'm not sure, but I think something is wrong."

When they returned to the banquet room, the waiter redirected our party to the special dining area … with the Queen-backed chairs! Mom asked, "What happened?"

The waiter smiled and replied, "I believe there was a mix-up in the seating!"

When we were all seated, and I was smiling again, Mom asked what had happened. I explained they tried to get away with seating us where they wanted, and I wasn't going to stand for it when I had made special arrangements for our special Mother's Day together.

Mom said, "I wasn't sure what was going on, but I could tell something was wrong when that lower lip pout came out on your face!" She added, "You used to do that as a child, when you were upset!"

We had a wonderful meal, after all - and very attentive waiters and managers, by the way! I was a very happy "kid!" And I think the special day was even more memorable for Mom because of my lower lip protruding when I was having my temper tantrum! It brought back some special memories for her. I just reached for another antacid!

The next day they left for the remainder of their trek to Seattle. I learned later in a card from Mom that when they arrived home, I was departing for the Greek Cruise vacation. They did not return their rental car, keeping it an extra day, so they would be available whenever I called to talk with them before the ship sailed. That's some caring parents!

A Greek Cruise Getaway ...

My two-week May vacation on a Greek Cruise was a tough time for Mom and Dad - and me too. It was the first time we would be out of communication for any length of time since we had reunited. Mom was sad but wanted to be brave so I would have a good time.

I actually took pictures of Mom and Dad along with me, so I could picture them in my mind during my time away; our acquaintance was too new for me to be able to remember exactly what they looked like without a visual aid!

They were thoughtful to send a message to the ship's stateroom to tell me to, "Have a great time!" They were genuinely happy for me to have a nice vacation, as opposed to the guilt trips I had been raised on.

The cruise was excellent ... scenery was as beautiful as the pictures show in travel brochures; weather was lovely; food and entertainment on board ship were terrific; shore excursions were educational and interesting! The two weeks rest was successful in giving me a positive attitude adjustment!

On the way home from the cruise, upon landing in New York, I phoned home to tell Mom and Dad I'd see them soon. At that moment, I noticed I had lost the opal stone from the ring Mom had given me. I really got upset and Dad detected it right away. He asked me what was wrong. I told him what had just happened; it must have happened in the restroom stop I made. He said, "Don't worry about it! And don't let it disturb your vacation happiness! We'll get you another stone when you get here!" Can you believe he would be so understanding?! That was just what he did too … as soon as I got to the house and unpacked, off we went to the jewelers!

Father's Day Surprise …

I told Mom I wanted to surprise Dad on Father's Day. She thought that was a great idea and was good at keeping a secret.

My flight arrived very early that morning and I took a taxi over to the condo. I was waiting in the kitchen talking with Mom, while Dad was still sleeping.

When he was waking up, she suggested he put on some shorts over his night underwear. But he objected saying, "Why should I do that? I never do that until after breakfast."

She didn't push it. So, out he comes in his underwear … and I say, "Hi Dad! Happy Father's Day!" Because I knew Mom tried to convince him otherwise, I chided, "Don't you dress up for guests?"

Well, I learned he was a blusher! He looked at Mom and said, "Why didn't you tell me we had company?"

She said, "It was a surprise!"

"Oh my! I guess so!" he said. "Excuse me while I get some clothes on!"

But he was very happy I came to make his Father's Day special. It was certainly a day I never thought I'd be honoring again in my lifetime.

Dad informed me that I had replaced his daughter, Karyn, in his life. He said God had given me to him as his daughter too … not just to Mom. That was a pretty special feeling.

Some Criticism to Handle …

I went to see some Ohio friends who were visiting Southern California. They had sent me pictures of my father and mother's wedding. I was so happy to share with them the success of Mom's and my reunion and pictures from that reunion weekend.

What I didn't expect was the feedback I received … not realizing that these friends of my father and stepmother were still very loyal to them. My friends told me not to think unkindly toward my father and stepmother; to realize there is more to the stories than I was hearing; to remember the good from all the years I was with my father and stepmother. They said to let bygones be bygones.

I couldn't do what they were saying. They hadn't lived in the home I grew up in. This visit totally depressed me. I can't dwell on the possibility that I don't have the full story on any of my mother's situation … because then I'm back to judging, which God told me not to do.

I saw Beverly the next day and questioned if I had to go through these feelings every time I met someone from my past who disagreed with my go-forward plans. She gave me some advice, but I needed time to absorb how to handle the criticism.

When Mom called me, she asked what was wrong. I told her I had a therapy session and was still sorting out the advice I had been given. She reminded me I could say anything I needed to say or ask of her, and that I shouldn't worry about hurting her feelings. I told her I didn't care what the past was. I loved her and always will.

Apparently, I was not quite ready to deal with the hurtful stories people might tell. So, maybe I wasn't ready to meet the relatives yet either. These friends have a right to their opinions, but I have a right to mine; they didn't live what I did. Besides, God had ordered me to find Mom and forget the past; I had to obey that instruction, in spite of friends' opinions or viewpoints.

I had to work through some of these feelings with prayer and visiting with friends who provided some good counsel. I spoke more with Mom. We agreed to just keep pressing on, in spite of knowing we had missed much in each other's lives.

Some Creative Fun During Our Visits …

When I would visit Mom and Dad, I took over updating the decorations on the kitchen table and changing the theme at least once a month. One time I did a beach scene; another time a good luck theme; a holiday or birthday theme for appropriate months.

I used knickknacks or collectibles Mom had around the house for the displays. Mom told me anything I wanted to use was fine with her. What freedom! I thought maybe Mom would object to my moving things around to do the displays or feel badly that I changed the scenes. But on the contrary, she was happy to see my creativity - and believed it must have come from her genes! Dad even got into it sometimes and gave me ideas.

Even though many of the stuffed bears now 'lived at other addresses' to make room for me at Mom and Dad's, several were still around for me to 'play' with. I'd display some of the bears in a funny scene for Mom and Dad to wake up to - while I was still sleeping in from the "red eye" flight. When Mom wasn't feeling good on one occasion, I had the bears giving first aid to the "sick" bear. Another time, when Mom had a sore foot from a podiatry visit, all the bears "found out" and had their left feet bandaged the next morning, just like Mom did! When she came home from the hospital one time, all the bears were modeling the latest in "hospital gown fashions!" Mom and Dad found my humor fun and appreciated my efforts to keep them smiling!

The bears all had names, compliments of Mom. They would leave messages using their names, like Floppy, Schlock, Grumpy, or Pooky. The messages I'd find in my suitcases or briefcase on trips home would be from one of the bears. When a message was about one of the bears, it was written and signed by "Grandma." These always made me smile!

Sometimes my bedroom would have a banner saying something like, "Welcome Home!" signed "All the Bears – We Missed You!"

Anytime we decorated the house for special occasions, the bears were involved too! I wish the bears could have actually blown up the balloons I had bought, because I thought I was going to blow out a lung trying to do those manually in order to decorate for "Grandpa's" birthday! We had a space ship theme and the bears did a good job dressing appropriately and "going where no bear had gone before!"

Mom's cards and notes would sometimes come addressed to Mom's "grandkid," Cricket, from the bears. Or Mom would send cards saying, "Give a pat to Cricket," or to "Ms. C." This was the start of a very unique relationship between Mom and her 4-legged "grandkid." Mom and Cricket eventually became good buddies as fortunately Mom ended up not being allergic to Cricket for some miraculous reason. That was a blessing for all of us!

One trip I decided to convert an empty flower basket into a "lighthouse" because I was a lighthouse collector! I added a light bulb to it with duct tape - no electricity, but any lighthouse needs a light! It was named "the Cove Cay Lighthouse," founded in 1997, and assigned some of the bears to look after its maintenance and improvements! Mom and Dad didn't want me to take it down when I left town; they would laugh about it when I wasn't there.

We had fun with these humorous activities. Some of it may seem childish, but remember I was never able to enjoy a real childhood. Earlier in my life, no one would have appreciated these attempts at humor. These activities proved to be very healing for me - and for Mom and Dad.

What Was Mom Feeling ...

Mom wasn't openly communicative about how she felt since we reunited. I received plenty of cards telling me she loved me and showing me her wonderful sense of humor. But it isn't the same as really telling me what she felt from her heart about everything. So, I asked her if she would write me a letter explaining her feelings about our reunion, our life together since the reunion, the missing years, and anything else on her heart. These are Mom's words verbatim from a letter mailed to me on July 19, 1997:

Hi Baby Girl:
You wanted to know how I feel about the changes in my life since Feb 9th. So here goes as best I can explain myself.

I, like you, have mixed emotions - highs and lows.

The biggest problem I have is dredging up old painful memories of my first marriage. I have two consolations - one a lovely daughter who I have always loved and of course love as much as an adult as I did when she was younger.

The second consolation is I gave my 1st marriage my "best shot." I tried for 7 years purely one-sided to make my marriage work. I was afraid of your father and his temper - he did everything to destroy my self-esteem and darned near succeeded. Had I been alone I would have left him long before I did. But having you to care for was a huge responsibility and not to be taken lightly - that is what prompted me to go to your grandparents. I felt they loved you and although they weren't too aware of our marital problems had seen your father's temper on occasion - also knew the problem of his family coming first over you.

When I look back now to that time, I realize I did the only thing I could to preserve my sanity. Physically my blood pressure was sky-high; my nerves were shot and I could see no future. Several things indicated your father would never change - as I told him he needed nothing more than a housekeeper and a woman in bed (note the term wife was not used.)

Now let's fast forward to my being notified of your adoption. We sent depositions to the California Judge who did nothing but type on the back: Adoption Granted. None of us saw the actual adoption papers. At this point I went into a mental tailspin. Your Dad had been supportive of me from the beginning - but now took over as Doctor - Counselor - and husband. Our marriage has had a lot of bumps in it but this was a terrible ordeal for us. We can't say our attorney had not warned us the case would play out exactly as it did. He said, "California takes care of its own."

I don't know what "co-dependency" is according to Beverly. In my book it is being there for someone in need - no thought to anything other than standing by to help and William F (my step-dad) was right there. It took several months for me to respond - but he wouldn't leave me alone to pine away. He forced me back into the human race I wanted to drop out of. He is now and always will be (and has been in the past) my greatest gift from God. (Not born to me).

For me to have marriage #1 - 7 years of hell and then be blessed for the next 44 years (& it isn't over yet) of mutual respect - being termed the Perfect Woman who never makes a mistake - enjoying life to its fullest - and being loved and cherished is more than any woman could ask for.

Healing took some time - your Dad encouraged me to go out - get involved - make speeches - always there for me - what a contrast!

The only way for me to achieve positive results was to put marriage #1 out of my mind. Never mention it to anyone - and of course not tell anyone about you.

(This part of the letter was written two days later.)

Janet, this is a **very** difficult letter to write. Like your Dad said today we've talked more about ECT (my father) this past couple of months than ever in our entire married life. I don't want to poison your mind about your father - so I'll say no more about that part of my life. (I'm really not that noble - it is just too upsetting for me even after all these years).

For us to have you as part of our family after all these years is beyond belief. And for us all to get along so well is even more incredible.

Again this goes back to WFW (my step-dad) and NEW's (my Mom's) love for each other. What I did for Karyn I did because she was his daughter. I loved her "warts & all" and feel she loved me the same way. It gives me a comfortable feeling to know we did our best for her & I never resented her - we were always there for her & will always be there for you.

It hurts when I look back & know I could have been a part of your early years as WFW was a part of Karyn's. It does work. Why we didn't have that I don't know & I feel cheated because of it. Not to see you graduate - your prom dress - even back to grammar school. But that is in the past. We can't undo that but we can make the rest of our lives count.

Does it hurt to hear you call Elizabeth Mom? Of course it does - no one should have been allowed to take my rightful place! But she did & you obviously had a deep affection for her or you wouldn't still be in grief counseling. I can't tell you that goes away quickly either. Your Dad & I still have trouble over Karyn's death - 13 years later! So you have to have patience - remembering the good times will help!

You will be a big help to us now - I guess you know that by now.

I hope you can share our lives - learn to laugh more. Get out & enjoy life like you should have done all along. You don't owe anyone anything ("You've paid your dues") and now it's your turn.

When I had you, I thought you were a miracle and now that we've met again, I still think you are a miracle.

I wish we lived closer together, but am delighted that we can visit via letter and phone. That's more than I had for 45 years, and I'll gladly settle for that.

Janet, remember I went through a tough pregnancy and never regretted it because you were such a cute baby (hair or no hair!) You were mine - I fought for you then and will fight for you now.

I love you Baby - and Dad and I are here for you.

Mom

It was a difficult letter for her to write and is still an emotional one for me to read. I'm so happy I asked her to write this, so I could be sensitive to certain feelings and hurts she was experiencing as our intimate relationship continued to mature.

Some Things to Change ...

In July, Dad mentioned to me that he's glad Mom's so happy, but added that, "finally we're talking about something besides you," meaning I've been the main topic of conversation for the past five months. That signaled to me that he missed the life he and Mom had before I came on the scene.

I used an opportunity later that day alone with Mom to encourage her to be more sensitive to Dad's needs - like she used to be. Mom understood what I meant. The ability to discuss anything, anytime, and anyway with Mom, without fear of criticism or condemnation, was a wonderful freedom I now had.

This was a signal to me too not to build my whole life around Mom and Dad. They had been encouraging me to make more friends than just them, so "when they are gone I won't be alone." That was a bitter thought to swallow, but a kind encouragement on their part.

Concentration on work and cultivating more friendships on the West Coast became stronger points of focus for me after this. I would still see Mom and Dad at least once a month and talk with Mom daily. But I gave some space and less intensity to our relationship in the later months of 1997.

More Ups and Downs ...

Just when I think we've made progress, something happens that takes me back to reality.

We had a good weekend together for Labor Day. Sunday church was good as usual. We visited with an ever-expanding group of Mom and Dad's friends who I was getting to know with each of my Clearwater visits. We had lunch with some friends on Sunday afternoon. On Monday, we went to breakfast with other friends at a favorite restaurant overlooking the water. Then, drove to Tampa for a lunch barbeque and swim at Carol's.

That night, I hugged Mom before bed and said, "I wish I'd been able to hug you like this for the past 40 years, but it feels good now."

That's when I saw the hurt in her eyes, as she said, "I still can't go there or think at all about that, it hurts too much."

As I'm trying hard to focus on what God's given me going forward, I lose sight that Mom's still got a lot of hurts, un-forgiveness, and unexplained events that continue to haunt her. I pray God will be able to help heal those hurts as He's helping me daily with mine.

Anniversary Wishes to Mom and Dad ...

Due to my budget constraints, I found a more creative and less costly way to give something to Mom and Dad on special occasions. After only knowing and observing them for 9 months, I wrote the following tribute and framed it for their 44th wedding Anniversary on September 26th, 1997:

Marriage Between Friends

Never have I observed first-hand a marriage based first on friendship, then on love ... that is until I met Norma and Bill Wallace, my mother and step-dad, in February 1997.

Forty-four years after this friendship began, they are still best friends. This friendship appears to be built on several things: mutual respect, always giving the other person more credit for successes, good communication, not focusing on failures, never tearing down, always building up the other person. Sounds like the Love Chapter (1 Corinthians 13) come to life, doesn't it?

Philosophically, I've heard that marriages are always based on give-and-take, but now I've witnessed it working best when each just concerns themselves with giving.

In the first conversation I had with Mom after forty-five years, she told me there are two kinds of love - just being loved or truly being cherished. Mom said she was "truly cherished." I've seen Dad consistently consider Mom's needs before his own. Dad's especially happy if he sees Mom happy. Not many men would give so much credit for a successful marriage to their wife - but Dad does. He's not proud, she's not demanding; they're just best friends. I suspect it's because of these unselfish positions that their beautiful marriage proceeds down the path of success. No magic ... but true giving; not demanding their own way; not focusing on the tough times, about what was overcome or sacrificed, but learning and working through hard times, hand and hand; and making the other's happiness more important than their own.

In a time when one out of two marriages fails, it's important to consider what makes a marriage truly successful. I'm grateful to be a witness to a forty-four year success story between two best friends ... my Mom and Dad!

Happy Anniversary
Love, J'Gay

They appreciated the sentiments and said it was more valuable to them than any gift I could have given. I know they were biased, but it made me happy to make them happy.

The Roller Coaster Continues ...

Mom and Dad had been wonderful about taking me into their lives and home; they made me feel greatly loved and welcome. Even their second daughter, Carol, made me feel welcome each time I talked or visited her.

Mom and Dad recognized things I like, or do, that are different from their routines; and sincerely wanted me to do what I'd like, whenever I wanted to. They wanted me to always feel like their home was my home too.

I felt comfortable and excited to visit them now, and I was not as sad as I used to be when I had to leave them. Guess we did well "getting acquainted" through all the visits and phone calls.

Mom made me special White Chocolate and Macadamia Nut cookies for my late October visit, along with another yummy Pineapple Upside-Down cake! She knows how to make me feel special and spoiled!

During the October visit, I learned that Dad hadn't been feeling well and his illness concerned me. I suggested it might be a medicine change needed; but he wouldn't tell the doctor how sick he felt. Mom was really worried about his being in more pain than normal.

Dad brought up an upsetting topic for me … about the possibility of his dying before Mom, which made me know he didn't feel well at all.

Mom talked with me this weekend about "not being able to go on without him," and about her and Dad being able "to go together like in an accident or something."

That was too **hard** for me to face then! If I didn't care about them both, it wouldn't be so difficult to face these possibilities. But I was attached to this "family" already. I prayed God would find something to improve Dad's health and, in turn, keep Mom healthy for a long time to come!

These thoughts and other topics I discussed with Mom made me sad this trip. It was apparent that Mom's continuing sadness was still there. She told me people asked her if I remembered anything of the years I was with her as a child. But I didn't. The thought that almost all of my memories of her were non-existent increased her sadness.

She reminisced about an incident shortly before I was kidnapped. I had run out in front of a bus and she spanked me, so I'd remember NOT to do that again. I don't recall that incident or consequence. But Mom feared that was one of the last things I might have remembered about her. She felt sad about it all those years I was missing. Her thinking that might have been my last memory of her for all those years just makes me want to cry.

I keep telling myself I have to go on and not think about the lost years for Mom's and my sake. While I know that's logical and ordered by the Lord, sometimes a stray, sad thought creeps in. Just today, the Scripture reading in church triggered sad thoughts and made them hard to overcome.

Mom had eye surgery shortly after I left town in September. I spoke with her that night. She was ordered to bed rest, but the doctor felt it would be successful.

When I encouraged Dad again to go to the doctor, he refused until his regularly scheduled January visit - which was three months from now!

I found myself growing more concerned with their health problems. All I could do was pray for their healing - and take my migraine medicines!

Mom's Birthday Surprise …

In my October Clearwater visit, I wanted to pick up Mom's birthday gift I had ordered in advance from her favorite jeweler for her mid-November birthday. Just in case it wasn't what I wanted or needed tweaking, I wanted to check on the gift this trip. To keep it a surprise, I asked Dad to ride with me under the guise of getting my every-day jewelry checked for any loose stones.

The gift was perfect! The jeweler wrapped it and placed it in a lovely gift bag. On the way back from the jewelry store, Dad asked me, "Do you want to know how to drive your mother nuts?"

I wasn't sure if the right answer to that question was "Yes" or if I was taking it too seriously by thinking "Absolutely not!" But I went along with him, when I saw the smile on his face, and commented, "Sure, what do you have in mind?"

"Show your mother the bag," he said. "Tell her it's for her birthday, but that she can't open it until November 15. Put the gift bag on top of the entertainment center (which was above the living room TV, so she would be looking at it daily!), it will drive her nuts to not know what's in it!"

"That's mean!" I said, but was intrigued because he was having fun with the idea. "Don't you think she'll open it and re-close it?" I asked.

He said, "Absolutely not!"

So, that's what we did. Then, Dad teased her about it all day while she "pouted." She was so curious. But she did wait until I returned for her November 15th birthday to open that surprise!

That trip the "bears" decorated the house the night before her birthday. Mom wanted to open her gift immediately when she woke up - enough of the waiting! She loved all of her gifts. I can't recall which special gift I gave her that year, but I sure remember Dad having the pleasure of teaching me how Mom loves surprises and driving her nuts in the process!

Carol came over with a homemade cake. We all went to "The Beachcomber" for lunch. We had a great "family" celebration for Mom's 72nd birthday.

A Traditional "Family Project" ...

Around Thanksgiving each year, I get my Christmas cards ready for a December 1st mailing. I usually do individual notes in each card, so it takes some time to compose a personal note, address the cards, label and stamp them. Mom offered for her and Dad to help me! Who was I to refuse their welcome help!

Dad couldn't believe the number of cards I send and asked if I just sent one out to everyone I ever knew! He was teasing about it all the time we worked on what was referred to as "a family project."

Mom was quietly addressing the envelopes, while Dad was complaining about what was taking me so long with my part of the "family project!"

I told him, "Big deal! All you do is put on the stamps and labels! It takes time to write these notes!"

That became a fun family tradition every year ... and each time I could think up a "family project" for us to do collectively! I can still hear him say, "Oh my!" and roll his eyes when I'd announce, "Time for a family project!"

Holiday Celebrations 1997 ...

Mom, Dad, Carol and I enjoyed a Thanksgiving dinner together at the Country Club.

We made a visit to Sarasota the day after.

Then, Carol and I worked on decorating Mom and Dad's condo with the many Christmas decorations they had to display. (We could have used the "bears" help, but I think they were hibernating from too much Thanksgiving food!) This "decorating party" would become another traditional "family project!"

A large volume of work projects in process, West Coast family obligations, and personal relationships took up much of December, until I was able to return to Clearwater for a 10-day vacation for the Christmas season.

One of the downsides to any holiday was the selection of greeting cards for Mom and Dad. Do you know how many card verses for close family members imply they have been there for you your entire life?! I could start shopping for a card and end up in a very sad or angry mood.

Other than the card selection difficulty, I can't put into words how wonderful this Christmas was for me! I felt very fortunate and blessed by the Lord to have Mom and Dad's unconditional love for me and their wise counsel at my disposal; I had special West Coast friendships to feel good about; a job that was challenging but had good benefits and a future that looked bright; and for the first time in my life I was really only responsible for me.

Christmas with my new family was time for a new "family tradition!" This was met with some objection, but not too strenuous. I preferred to open presents on Christmas morning. This was breaking the family tradition of opening gifts on Christmas Eve. My logic was Christmas Eve was Dad's birthday ... so we had to properly recognize and acknowledge that special event before we had our Christmas celebration!

The Christmas gift exchange was special, all gifts greatly appreciated. Mom gave me a collector's doll. I had told Mom I couldn't remember having a doll as a child, except for the memory I had of the shelf of dolls she had for me as a baby. I still have that beautiful collector doll as a reminder of her love expressed during our first Christmas together in 45 years. They also gave me anything I ever expressed an interest in and more!

I made a plaque for Mom and Dad as one of my Christmas gifts to them. It really did capsulize all of our feelings, I believe. Dad had to finish reading the plaque aloud because Mom was crying too hard:

Our First Christmas
1997

Most 50-year old "kids" can't remember their "first" Christmas. At 50, they are lucky to even remember to phone home … considering other priorities, distances, or disabilities.

50-year olds certainly don't believe in Santa anymore. They are too grown up to sit on Santa's lap (at least in public!), too sophisticated to ask for toys they'd probably enjoy, and too cost-conscious to buy themselves what they really want. But they're always willing to find just a little extra for one more gift for a friend, or to provide a meal for the homeless, or to give something from "Santa's Helper" for a needy child.

These "kids" make lists - because their memories aren't what they used to be! The lists are checked twice to be sure gifts in mind would be welcomed by the recipients, or that recipients are even still around to receive them! Then, a furious pace is set to shop, wrap gifts, send cards, mail packages, decorate, bake, deliver gifts and holiday goodies, attend a few parties or family gatherings, and try not to forget what the holiday truly means.

Only when slowed down for a seasonal church service, does a "kid" focus on what started all these traditions so long ago. During such quiet moments, thoughts turn to home, family, friends, and the fond memories they all tend to create.

For this "kid," her 50th Christmas will be a "FIRST" to always be remembered! Family takes on new meaning and new looks. Home is now bi-coastal ... with shorts the standard dress in winter. The preparations are made with utmost concern for the "kid's" wants and desires - not only with "needs" in mind. New traditions make touching memories that neither distance, nor time, will ever erase. Wrapped packages bring as much joy and intrigue as their actual contents. The giving is from hearts filled with unconditional love poured into each action. The calendar goes too fast as time together becomes more precious each day.

Feeling the love and passing it on are important gifts to exchange this year. Filling hearts with 45 years of laughter and joy, instead of more tears, is high on our Christmas lists. Acceptance of the unchangeable past becomes our gift to ourselves. And living NOW to the fullest becomes what we all want for Christmas.

Christmas 1997 will never be again ... except as OUR FIRST for this 50-year old "kid." Thanks, Mom and Dad, for creating and sharing such special memories ... our memories ... of this holiday season.

Love, J'Gay

After Christmas, Mom asked me to take down the Christmas decorations for them. I was very happy to help with that. They were so relieved to have the help you'd have thought I gave them the moon! But Dad wasn't feeling his best and it was too much for both of them to face for New Year's when they normally do it.

We didn't do anything else special, just visited and rested. The bears did their usual nighttime displays with notes to "Grandma" each morning.

It's wonderful that Mom and Dad want nothing from me. They enjoy my love and give theirs freely to me. They are always happy for me, make suggestions or give their viewpoint, but are sensitive to not tell me what to do. No one could ask for better parents or friends, nor ask to be treated better than they treat me.

I had to leave for home and work the next day ... but I knew when I'd be coming to my "second home" again ... and that made leaving a bit easier.

Mom Says It All …

I received this note when I arrived back home after Christmas and was blessed:

> Hi Honey:
>
> I wonder if you know how much it means to have my baby in my arms, not only for Christmas but for your birthday, Mother's Day, (and every day).
>
> I have longed for this even though Dad and I have our special marriage, but you were always missing and I would ask God to take care of you wherever He looked in on you. My prayers were answered because you are a special "kid" and I love you "this much"!
>
> Thank you for your gifts, but thank you also for making time in your life to see us. You are the greatest!
>
> I love you - I looked at you last night and you are mine! We're going to have a great life now, a little late, but let's enjoy what we have.
>
> I love you - little girl.
>
> Mom - & Dad too!

Happy "Old" Year 1997 …

What kind of year it was for me?

Amazing
Step-by-step, it was ordered by the Lord.
Each day we could be together was priceless!
Lessons learned caused changes in life's priorities.

Healing
I can't change the past; I must move on!
I don't want to misjudge any longer.
I'm loved by "Mama & Papa Bear."
No one will be allowed to take advantage again.

Transforming

The touch of mother's unconditional love is priceless!
Nothing will cause my mother to not love me!
I found joy unspeakable and true happiness!

* * * * * * *

Would I want to do it all over again?
> NO … it was too emotional and tiring.

Was it worth it?
> YOU BET!

If I could change anything, what would it be?
> I can't change anything, so why dwell on it!

What have I learned?
> What haven't I learned!

* * * * * * *

Happy "New" Year 1998 …
With more life changes to come …

Chapter 5

MORE LIFE-CHANGING EVENTS

"Be anxious for nothing, but in everything, by prayer
and supplication with thanksgiving, let your
requests be made known unto God."
Philippians 4:6

Health issues would become a greater obstacle for us to overcome than the strenuous travel schedule, which continued for the next two years.

The pain of our missing years eased some as we experienced several family crises that helped us focus on "today!" It was a turning point for me to stop looking back ... and get on with what I had, as God had instructed me. It was just going to take some serious times for me to finally get the message! I wish I didn't always need a WHOMP on the head for God to get my full attention!

But first ... there were some special times to celebrate.

First Year Reunion Anniversary ...

January 9, 1998, was the one-year anniversary of God telling me to find Mom. I sent Mom flowers for recognition of that special day ... and thought, "WOW! What a life-changing year it has been!" She and Dad agreed!

It had been a very tough year of personal adjustments, financial struggles, settling my stepmother's estate, heavy business travel, work assignment demands, working on some side businesses I had developed, and fitting in extra visits to Clearwater. It was almost too much for too long, as all took their toll on health; but the gains were worth it!

The sermon at church the week of January 9 happened to be on Leviticus 25 and 26, which speaks of the 50th Jubilee year. It truly and literally was my 50th Jubilee year ... I was enjoying abundance after bondage, and freedom and forgiveness after tough times. It was a wonderful revelation. I needed to remember that the good things are dependent on obedience to God and make sure I keep Him in the right priority!

> For our January 9th First Contact Anniversary, Mom selected a card that said, "You came, falling like a miracle into my life, filling my heart with beautiful dreams and wishes. To tell you, on this our special day, that you are ... and always will be ... **my love.** Happy Anniversary." She wrote, "My Baby, You were a miracle to me the 1st time and are still a miracle! I love you "this much" and so does Dad. Your Mother"

I was able to be with Mom and Dad for the actual one-year Reunion Anniversary. To commemorate this special day, February 9, I wrote Mom a message and framed it. Both Mom and Dad liked it well enough to hang it among the other framed gifts I'd given them:

Our First Reunion Anniversary

The year started with a phone call ... one that would change some lives forever. Questions of a lifetime would be answered, finally. Daily communications would add to truth and understanding. The exchanges re-bonded the lives forced apart long ago. An unforgettable experience of unconditional love had begun.

There were many moments of special sharing ... always tempered with honesty and caring. Tears flowed freely as layers of hurt, sadness, and disappointment were explored. Much was learned about each other ... about life lived ... and about life missed. There were exciting times to share, others were too sad for words. There were plenty of laughs and much heartache. But most importantly, there was always love ... in each thought, word, and deed.

I learned I could love again … and be loved. Doubts and fears fled. I felt the touch of my mother's hand in love, and her hugs have made my world right again. Daily support and encouragement have replaced past hurts and criticism. The empty spot in my heart is filled. The strength of her love, the confidence she will always love me, the wisdom of her advice, and the softness of her touch are now among my special treasures.

Each day new memories are made. Each day more love and joy are exchanged. Each day more healing happens and more freedom is mine. Each day I'm richer and happier than ever before.

A whole New World has opened to me … led by God … step by step. And now … one year later … it truly is a …

> VERY HAPPY REUNION ANNIVERSARY!
> Mom, I love you THIS MUCH!
> J'Gay
> 2/9/98

Mom and Dad had a floral arrangement delivered to their church, and dedicated in honor of our Reunion Anniversary. Their pastor spoke on Luke 5, and mentioned, "how God can turn the ordinary into extraordinary, like a phone call from a daughter can change a life!"

For our First Reunion Anniversary, Mom wrote me a card saying, "What a great year this has been for us! And God willing - many more to come. Please remember I love you "this much" and that will never change! You are mine forever. I would not change that for anything. And the icing on the cake is Dad loves you too. Your Mother"

Mom started adding "LCA" to the cards after her signature … standing for "Love Conquers All" - and truly it was helping us day by day.

Before I returned to California, the front table was redecorated with a Valentine's Day theme. And since the Olympics were on then, the bears did a sports scene of the "First Cove Cay Bear Olympics!" Mom and Dad enjoyed both efforts … and I enjoyed making their day brighter.

Significant Work Changes Made ...

Just before the First Reunion Anniversary trip to Clearwater, some major organizational changes were made at work. It took some time to see advantages to the job and reporting structure changes. These were probable answers to my prayers, and would enable me to handle job pressures and workload better.

The feeling had been growing that work was a secondary priority for the first time in my life. I knew that was difficult for my employer to accept after it being first priority for almost 25 years. They had a business to run with demands greater than ever before. But I now had a life besides that employer.

For all the company did over the three years of our "reunion and get acquainted" times, to allow me to travel and work remotely, I'll forever be grateful.

In retrospect, I believe God was preparing me for upcoming life changes that would take place. Pride kept getting in my way, but eventually the Lord helped me accept the changes and succeed because of them.

Mom and Dad knew these organizational changes were tough for me to accept. They were probably much wiser than me about what the changes signified. So, they spent some time discussing with me the possibilities of early retirement, at 55 rather than 65. They were even considering ways they could help financially make that happen. That gave me something unexpected to consider and look forward to. At this stage, I believed I could do 4 more years - just wasn't so sure about 14 more years!

As it turned out, I didn't use the alternative, but it was a nice thought to dwell on when the days ahead got tough!

Continuing to Keep In Touch ...

Sharing time daily by phone with Mom was still an important priority. But each of us committed to keeping our lives going while on opposite Coasts.

Mom and Dad were still reluctant to fly to California due to health issues. So, when I could schedule a trip to Clearwater, their schedules were cleared to allow for my visit or they just included me in their "family" plans.

We still spent lots of time during every visit talking rather than sightseeing. Getting to know **them**, not Florida, was my main goal.

I would still visit as often as business travel and vacation times allowed. It averaged 1 or 2 trips per month, spending 89 days with them in 1998 during

19 trips, and 113 days during 21 trips in 1999. The increasing number of days was due to growing health concerns.

Learning More Every Visit …

Mom and Dad wanted me to have whatever collectibles of theirs I wanted. I said, "That's fine when the time comes, but not now."

But they insisted that I be able to enjoy the glassware while they were still alive, if I liked any of it. I didn't like what this discussion signaled. To me, it meant they were planning for the end times and I didn't want to face that topic.

My point of compromise was to write down the history of each collectible. I'm a "sentimental slob" and if I knew a piece came from my mother, grandmother or great-grandmother, it was more important to me than something someone gave them who I didn't know. To this day I still have that list of family history … along with many of the lovely collectibles.

I learned much more about Mom's occupations as our time together continued. Mom's first boss in Florida banking, her long-time friend, Carl, filled me in on the kind of employee she was. Mom had been the Head Teller and Assistant Cashier at Gulf-to-Bay Bank when she first worked for Carl.

He said many complimentary things about Mom such as she never forgot a name or a customer's personal situation they shared with her. Mom would be sure to greet a customer by name and maybe ask how their sick child was that the customer shared with her the previous visit. This type of recall made Mom very popular with bank customers. They would patiently wait in line for Mom to be their Teller. Carl would encourage people in the long line waiting for Mom to feel free to go to another Teller, but they would "insist on waiting for Norma."

Mom frequently had to use her sense of humor to diffuse sensitive situations. One time a salesman was trying to get Mom to go out to lunch with her, but Mom just kept telling him she was married. That didn't seem to matter to him! But it certainly mattered to Mom. So she told him about her mean, 300 pound, 6'5" husband, to finally discourage the guy. (Mean, Dad wasn't; protective and a big guy, he was!)

She was also known as the "fastest money counter" Carl had ever seen in his banking career.

I knew her as the only banker I could imagine who refused to have an

ATM card.

She felt money disappeared from your account too fast if it was too easily accessible. I can certainly vouch for that!

Mom had introduced the credit card program at the bank early in its inception, and always felt bad about how many young couples ended up in debt due to too many credit cards. I tried to explain that wasn't her fault and reminded her the economy depends on that kind of buying power. But she was still not happy about it.

Mom won a "Traveler's Checks" selling contest at the bank, sponsored by the credit card company. The prize was a TV that Mom wanted to have put into the employee lounge. Instead, the bank President kept the TV for himself! Mom never did forgive the President for that!

In another bank contest, Mom won a trip to Aruba for selling the most new accounts. She called Dad very excited about winning the trip, to which he replied, "Where the heck is Aruba?"

Mom said, "I don't know, but what do we care? It's free!" And they had a lovely time in that tropical locale.

Laughing More Every Visit ...

At Barnett Bank, Mom developed the "Newcomers' Program" to introduce new businesses in the area to the bank as prospective customers. As a marketing tool, she created a character called "Amazing Grace." Mom would dress up in this outfit and give her presentations: she wore a house dress with her slip longer than the dress, red-ribbed socks pulled half way up her calves, red high heels, a shower cap on her head with a mop head for hair, wore so much rouge and lipstick that one didn't recognize her (and Dad said, "Whatever you do, don't kiss me!"), carried a huge purse, and topped it off with a fox fur! When people got done laughing at her get-up, she'd have their undivided attention - and was top salesperson!

Ironically, she considered sending me that photo as the introductory picture of herself! I told her our reunion might never have happened and she had been afraid of that!!

However, since I had a similar creativity in business, being known for dressing in a bumble-bee outfit and as Minnie Pearl, complete with a hat out of cardboard and yelling a big "HOWDEE!!" ... I could totally understand and appreciate "Amazing Grace!" It was in the genes!!

One of the funniest stories Mom ever told was about some linoleum Dad got on sale. He thought it was a great opportunity to fix up their scaffolding business office in St. Louis. Dad asked Mom to help him with this installation.

As he started to unroll the linoleum, he found it curved up, rather than down ... so if he stretched it across the floor, it just rolled up behind him. It quickly became obvious why he got such a good deal on it!

So, Dad needed Mom to lie spread-eagled on the rolled out linoleum to hold it down while he tacked down the outside edges. As he left the room to get the hammer and nails, Mom was too lightweight to control the unrolled linoleum. It spun back up with her in the middle of it and her face pressed against it!!

She was trying to yell, "Will, HELP!" to Dad, which sort of came out "Wel, HEP!" because she was "smooshed" in the rolled up roll and couldn't enunciate very well!

When Dad returned to the room, he said, "Norm, what did you do?! I asked you to do one thing and look what you did instead?!" He was kidding, of course, and very concerned that she wasn't injured. But it must have been a funny and helpless sight!

He modified the approach, tacking down just a little on one side at a time, and I know he didn't buy any more linoleum from that guy!

Falling into the category of "Mom never being able to get away with anything," she told me about this "one-of-a-kind" hand-painted tie that hung behind the door of Dad's office in Detroit. She couldn't recall him ever wearing it. When Mom's cleaning lady told Mom her husband had a special job interview and didn't have a tie to go with his sports coat, you know what Mom did! Yep ... gave her Dad's tie!

A few minutes later, Dad came in the office all upset saying, "Do you know what I just saw?! I just saw a man walking down the street wearing the same tie I paid $25 for that was supposed to be "one-of-a-kind"!"

What are the odds of Dad's coming back to the office, just as that man was walking away wearing Dad's tie?! Mom admitted that she had given his tie to the cleaning lady's husband for the interview and added, "besides, you never wear that tie!"

Of course, Dad said, "Well, I might have some day!" But he didn't mind. Remember he was always Mom's biggest fan - and she could do no wrong!

That is until he saw her teaching me how to play poker ...

While Mom was teaching me to play poker, I quickly learned that she and Dad were very lucky at cards. On the other hand, I had to have a "cheat-sheet" nearby to remember if a "flush" beat a "straight," or what "3 of a kind" beat!

When Mom would beat me badly at the game or raise the ante when she knew I didn't have a good hand, Dad would say to Mom, "Shame on you taking advantage of your daughter like that!" We'd all have a good laugh at that point. Every once in awhile though the cards would go my way, and then I was "merciless!"

The fun part for me was if you could win, it was acceptable to do so! When growing up, my stepmother was such a bad sport that I often had to force myself to lose in order to keep her happy. There's sure no fun in that!

We used to keep our change in plastic bags and pull it out if we wanted to bet quarters, dimes, or nickels on a hand. One day when the church kids were collecting coins for a mission project, we put our plastic bag of coins from the card playing activities into the offering.

The next week the head usher returned the plastic bag along with my "cheat-sheet!" I had forgotten it was in with the coins donated to the church. We had a good laugh over that -so did the head usher!!

I learned that Mom and Dad used to love to go fishing or hunting together for a getaway weekend. For someone who worried about how her hair looked, like I do today, it surprised me to consider Mom would do these outdoor activities, complete with hunting and fishing hats, in all forms of weather. She even baited her own hooks and helped with the fish cleaning. "Yuck!" was my comment. Commendably, Mom just loved being with the man she loved, and Dad didn't care what her hair looked like, just as long as they could get away together.

On this one occasion, they just got the boat out to the area of the river where they planned to fish for the day, when Mom discovered she needed to go to the bathroom badly. Dad advised her they couldn't go back to the lodge or they'd lose a half-day of fishing. So, he suggested she just hang herself over the boat edge and take care of business. Naturally, Mom questioned, "Right here in public??"

Dad responded, "No one's around way out here. Even if they do come nearby, we'll hear their engine and you can cover up quickly." It sounded like a good plan. So, feeling confident of Dad's assessment, Mom proceeded with the proposed process.

Just at that moment, out of the nearby bushes came a canoe, being paddled silently by a guide from their camp. The canoe glided quietly very close to Dad's boat! The guide was gentleman enough to just sail on by, not acknowledging that he had seen them!

Dad gulped and stuttered a little. Mom just laughed at the whole situation. Mom was sure the guide had a good story to tell over and over in the future … but hoped from the view he got he wouldn't be able to identify the exact party by name!

I could only imagine this "life's embarrassing moment" and have frequently laughed about it myself!

Mom explained that she hated to go to the dentist. She would make up excuses to not go, but Dad would follow up to be sure she kept her appointments. One time the dentist's office had been burglarized the previous night and hadn't been able to notify Mom until she arrived at their office of the need to cancel her appointment. When Dad called to check if she went, Mom gleefully explained that she couldn't "because of the burglary!" Can you imagine he didn't want to believe her?!

Mom finally admitted she preferred dentists to doctors, however, because they never weighed you! I could definitely relate to that!

Dad would sometimes give you a very detailed explanation about how to do something or how to get somewhere, which is why I could relate to this funny story Mom told.

Dad told Mom to be careful when she went out to the garage because the door between the kitchen and the garage could lock behind her if it closed. Mom thought, "Yah, yah " and wasn't really listening 100% to Dad's explanation.

In July, Dad left on a 10-day business trip to Germany. Mom finished a shower after working in the yard. She went into the garage … naked … to hang up the wet towels, when the door between the kitchen and garage shut behind her. At that moment, what Dad had told her registered … about being careful because the door would lock and she wouldn't be able to get back into the house without a key! One of life's darkest moments!

She thought, "I'm going to starve out here! There's no food and Will's gone 10 days! There are no clothes for me to put on and go to the neighbors and borrow the key they have. The car is here … but I can't be driving around naked! What do I do??!"

She located their previous year's Halloween costumes stored in the garage and donned the clown outfit. She opened the garage door and ran barefooted, in the clown costume, across the yard to the neighbors. When the neighbor answered, she said, "Don't ask questions, just give me the key to the house please!" She was rescued and thought she was home free!

When Dad returned, he asked how things went. She said, "Oh, fine. By the way, I had an extra key made and put it in the garage by the door between the kitchen and garage, and had a phone extension installed in the garage." Dad acknowledged those were great ideas!

At a cocktail party the following week, with Mom talking to one group of people and Dad with another, the Mayor, who lived across the street from Mom and Dad, yelled across the room to Mom inquiring, "Norma, what the heck were you doing running down the street in your clown outfit the other day?!"

Dad looked at Mom and said, "Everything went fine, eh?" Another good laugh!

Long Distance Health Issues …

I found there was no way I could let Mom or Dad be ill in Florida with me on the other side of the country. My heart just wouldn't let me do that.

If Mom was ill, Dad could hardly handle that crisis. Mom told me one time she had pleurisy, was down on the floor in pain, and asked Dad to call 9-1-1 to get an ambulance. He brought out the phone book and told her he didn't know where to look for it! He was just rattled when the love of his life took ill.

During one visit, Mom was crying after Dad went to bed. When I asked what was wrong, she was worried and troubled his mind was going. She didn't know if she could face it if he was developing Alzheimer's. I suggested it might be the physical pains he was struggling with; he had war injuries that were never addressed, shrapnel in both knees that you could feel protruding! That had to hurt terribly … but he stubbornly only took over-the-counter medicine. Plus, he was trying to stop smoking "cold turkey." I asked if she could encourage him to try a less severe approach to stopping the smoking or get stronger medicine from the doctor for the pain. Eventually, he did both.

With these kinds of health issues increasing, I knew I had to be there to provide some relief when I could. I knew there could be other jobs, but not other parents. Each day I had them was still very precious to me.

Mom Hospitalized ...

In April 1998, Mom was hospitalized with pneumonia. There was no way I could concentrate on my California work with her sick in Florida. When I spoke with Dad about Mom in the hospital, I could tell he was quickly growing weary.

With my bosses' understanding, I took another fast trip to Florida. I didn't tell Dad I was coming because I knew he would try to pick me up at the airport and had enough to worry about with Mom ill. So, I called my "Florida sister," Carol, who met my flight. We went straight to the hospital to see Mom. It was very early in the morning. Dad was still home sleeping.

As I was standing at Mom's hospital room door, she said, "Janet Gayle," and started crying, she was so happy to see me. She said she had just finished praying for help, and there I was standing at her door when she looked up. She said, "I was just dreaming about you! In fact, you were wearing the same thing you have on right now!" With all we'd been through, none of that surprised me!

I explained I had to come visit her to encourage her to get better soon and to help out Dad a little. She was grateful for that.

At a decent hour, we called Dad at home to check on him. Poor Dad! He was so upset that Mom wasn't well, he wasn't doing well himself. He was exhausted and not too alert when we called. Since he thought I was calling from California, he yelled at me, asking what I was doing up at that hour. We further confused him when Carol spoke with him, then Mom got on the phone, so he concluded we were on a conference call between California and Florida. When I explained I flew in to help, he said, "Oh my!" and was very relieved that help had arrived.

I did the driving to and from the hospital, and made sure Dad had food regularly and got some rest. I was worried we would need a room with two beds, if he didn't get on his feet better than he was!

Mom immediately began to improve shortly after I arrived. That night she left a voice message on the answering machine while we were in route back to the house that she was being held hostage, so to come back in the morning and rescue her! When she gets her sense of humor back like that, I know she's starting to feel better!

Unbelievably, the next morning she was ready to come home from the hospital. The doctor was surprised by her progress, but agreed to release her! Amazing progress!

I played "Nurse Jan" for a few days ... and both Mom and Dad were remarkably better by the time I had to return to work in California.

This was the first time I faced them being so ill and my being too far away to be able to help them. If my love for them wasn't creating enough pressure to make me want to be closer in proximity, this physical need certainly added to that desire!

I was jealous of the years we missed; I had trouble facing the prospect of losing Mom, or Dad for that matter. I realized how vulnerable they really are now versus just a year ago when I found them.

But reality mandated I return to work to keep making a living, and prayed they could continue being there for each other.

SSA Letter Finally Arrives ...

After 14 months, the letter arrived that I had written to the Social Security Administration (SSA) to be forwarded to Norma Wallace, now known as "Mom." Mom and Dad told me they cried when the letter arrived.

Mom asked if she could keep it if I didn't want it; I said certainly as long as it didn't make her sad.

Fortunately our reunion was a success. If it wasn't, this could have raised hurts all over again. But it was a risk worth taking at the time I wrote the letter to try to make initial contact using the SSA as an option.

Ohio Trip to See Relatives Postponed ...

I was planning a trip in May to finally meet my Cleveland, Ohio aunt, uncle, and cousins, as well as Dad's sister and niece in Cincinnati. Mom and Dad were going to go along with me. Mom runs the risk of being hurt from confronting the past or being confronted by my Cleveland relatives, but wants to be there so I don't get hurt in the process. "Mama Bear" looking after her young again! "Papa Bear's" going along to protect us both!

However, in mid-April, Mom was diagnosed with painful bursitis in both hips. Shots, exercise and therapy were prescribed for at least two weeks in order for her to get well.

Then, the call came in late April about her hospitalization with pneumonia.

On top of this, I was having knee problems. I had fallen on both knees the prior month during a business trip. The doctor's were debating if surgery was needed on my left knee, which continued to bother me.

It looked like God was not intending for us to go to Ohio right now, so I made the decision to postpone the trip to everyone's relief.

Mother's Day and Father's Day in Florida ...

I enjoyed both Mother's Day and Father's Day in Clearwater with Mom and Dad.

With Mom just recuperating from bursitis and pneumonia, we spent most of the Mother's Day weekend at home. But she did enjoy what I wrote for her and had imprinted on tulip (her favorite) stationery:

My Mother's Love

My Mother's love, so rich and free,
Kept through the years reserved for me.

I waited long to know her love;
God waited too in Heaven above.
The time was right. So finally ...
Her gift was shared abundantly.

Now her love is always there.
She treats me to her tender care.
We talk and plan and look ahead.
"Love's there no matter what!" she said.

Each day brings laughter; gone are tears.
Mother's love replaced my fears.
When thoughts of past o'erwhelm my soul,
Mom hugs me and says, "Let it go."

No matter what I think or say,
Her love is constant everyday.
There's nothing like her loving touch,
Showing me I'm loved "This Much!"
She prays for me, God's very best;
In His love and hers, I rest.
The time ahead is now our friend.

Our memories will have no end.

The past is gone. Its questions stay.
They're lost until Forever's day.
The healing came as love stepped in.
We both have let new lives begin.

It's true we've missed a lot down here,
But none can change what God's made clear:
My Mother's love, so dear to me,
Always there … Eternally!

Love THIS MUCH!
Happy Mother's Day 1998,
J'Gay

The words of this poem show how improved my thinking and living are now because of the year Mom and I have enjoyed together. I'm a blessed and spoiled "kid!"

> Mom sent me an Anniversary card in which she wrote, "The miracle of our reunion is only surpassed by our mutual respect and love for one another. You are my treasure and I love you this much!! Please don't dwell on the past when your future is so great! Freedom to do what and where you want is also a miracle for you. Be a good girl and remember we love you and are so proud of you! Mom & Dad"

These words reconfirm how my life has changed for the better! What great support and love Mom and Dad gave me.

For Father's Day, Dad commented to Mom, "I never thought I'd have another special Father's Day. But our little girl's being here is special!" Carol joined us for lunch at The Beachcomber. Then, we enjoyed some time for Bingo back at the house.

My Health in Jeopardy …

My health was worsening with the on-going stress. I was making bi-weekly visits to the chiropractor; my headaches were increasing again.

More re-organizational changes were made at work, which further lessened my workload. But instead of being accepting of this change, I felt guilty, like I should have been able to do it all.

I took some time with my counselor, Beverly, who explained that being unwanted and unloved for so long in my life made me an overachiever. I do it to try to gain acceptance. I needed to accept the job changes to enable some health improvements for me. Beverly counseled me about the different management style I was reporting into, and encouraged me to believe in myself because I knew the business and was still a valued employee.

Mom's Health Worsening ...

During my July trip to Clearwater, Mom was in great pain. She was seeing a specialist and facing possible surgery. Her hips were causing severe pain and the specialist wanted to try a series of more shots. I prayed God would enable her to walk normal and pain-free again.

God answered my prayer. The shots were successful and after weeks of therapy, Mom's hips were improving. After six months of problems, she was finally feeling better.

Attending a New Church ...

I started attending Puente Hills Baptist Church in Covina, California. They were a supportive and loving congregation. With all of the business and Clearwater travel, the pastor had been my "phone pal" more than I'd been able to regularly attend the church services. But Pastor Trisler had been a great encourager for me.

When Pastor Trisler asked for people to share their greatest answer to prayer, it gave me a chance to tell the abridged version about finding Mom. I explained that the reunion events were an answer to my prayer for God to give me back my joy. There weren't many dry eyes, including mine, as I realized just how miraculous it all was when I shared the story!

Pastor Trisler preached a sermon on "What Do You Do When Your Whole World Falls Apart?" He concluded with the statement that, "During these trials we may have the most intimate walk with the Lord."

That is what I have learned since God told me to find Mom in January 1997. It is a step-by-step walk and you have to keep close to Him, or you lose perspective and confidence.

Another Down Time Sneaks In ...

For a change, many things were going well in my life. I was feeling very positive on a business trip to the Northeast. Then, I went on to Mom and Dad's for a visit before another leg of the journey took me up North again.

During the Clearwater visit, I got depressed again about the past times I missed, times with Mom and Dad at events in their lives. As they talked about the past, I visualized the things I missed.

I talked about it with Mom, who is still having the same issues about my past that she missed. I cried and prayed about it all. I realized I can't go back, can't change the past, must move on, but am scared to in some ways. The future seems too uncertain yet.

I keep trying to enjoy each moment God has given us ... and limit the times I dwell on the past, although it seems to sneak in when I'm tired and vulnerable.

A Family Crisis ...

We were returning to Cove Cay, with Dad driving, Mom in the front passenger seat, Carol right behind Mom, and me behind Dad. Polite drivers were allowing us to cross the two lanes of stopped traffic to turn into the condo complex. All of a sudden, a car came up in the bus lane and broadsided "Big Red" at 40-50 mph.

I recall Mom saying, "Where did she come from? She's going to hit us!" And WOW! Did she ever!

I had the thought, "Why did that 3rd lane car speed up to hit us?" I didn't realize at that moment the 3rd lane was an illegal lane and the driver was trying to avoid all the stopped traffic by going around it. She didn't see us crossing into her path, while she was breaking the law.

Witnesses substantiated what had happened and called for help. Paramedics took us to the hospital in ambulances. Fortunately, we were all released that night. I had four staples for a cut in my head from hitting the roof. Mom had an injured arm and was very bruised. Dad had a knot on his forehead. Carol sustained the worst injuries of a broken collarbone in three places and required stitches to her one ankle.

It was frightening in retrospect to realize how disastrous that could have been! We were very blessed to have no loss of life. "Big Red" was totaled.

The next day we were naturally in even more pain, as more bruises and aches appeared. We spent the day trading ice packs, heating pads, and passing the Aspirin bottle.

As I was holding Mom's hand, crying a bit, I said, "I wondered how I'd ever live if something happened to you; but I didn't know how close we'd come yesterday to almost finding out!"

Thank God I was with them to help and try to support them through all of this, as opposed to being across the country.

The lesson I learned from this accident is that all we have is today. There's no guarantee of tomorrow. What is past is past; it needs to be let go. A strong lesson for me to learn and another WHOMP on my head to learn it! After this near-fatal accident, I am truly in the NOW!

Mom and Dad had to have transportation, so we went car shopping a few days after the accident. I had heard stories about what a terrific salesman Dad was, so I told him I hoped to learn some car buying strategy from his example.

We went to their regular car dealer and they found "Big Red II" immediately. It was another Lincoln Towncar, just like "Big Red" only with a caramel half-roof instead of white! I could tell Mom didn't want to even look one car further; she loved this one, just like she had loved "Big Red."

Now the negotiation lesson would begin! Momentarily, I thought maybe I should take notes, so I wouldn't forget how to handle this type of deal making in the future. But instead I decided to just quietly observe.

Dad asked how much the dealer wanted for the car and the salesperson told him the amount. Then, Dad said, "Okay, write up the contract!"

After the car salesperson left us, I questioned, "What kind of negotiating was that?! That's as good as I do!"

Dad said, "I knew your mother wanted this car. It was worth it to get her what she wanted. Besides, I know this dealership doesn't negotiate beyond the sticker price."

So much for that lesson! Actually, I think the lesson here is another example of Dad giving Mom just what makes Mom happy!! And that's an unforgettable lesson all by itself!

During a subsequent trip I made to Clearwater, the trial was held for the car accident. The driver of the car that hit us was found guilty; Dad was totally exonerated. I'm so glad that got resolved and I was able to be there for it. The guilty party's insurance company had some settlement issues to address.

Leave of Absence Needed ...

I traveled home after a few days of recuperation, only to have my Crockpot fall off the top of the refrigerator onto my right foot. Man, did that ever hurt! I used ice on it, but it got progressively worse. My podiatrist thought the foot was bruised or possibly chipped so he wanted it immobilized for the weekend. Can you imagine surviving a 50 mph car crash only to get clobbered in my own kitchen?!

Within two weeks, migraines were increasing and I had symptoms of a seizure coming on. The neurologist said they were due to the head trauma of the car accident. The chiropractor said my back and neck were bad before the accident and worse since. Both doctors were recommending time off from work to rest and recuperate. My boss agreed and suggested I recover in Clearwater, so I wouldn't be alone in case there were seizures.

Just before that Leave of Absence, I celebrated my 25th anniversary with the company. The lunch, the gift, and the speeches acknowledging accomplishments were nice to have.

By late September, I was heading to Clearwater on a Leave of Absence for two weeks. The only problem was Hurricane George was threatening the area. Fortunately, my flight didn't get cancelled, although those later than mine did. Arriving at Cove Cay, I learned that Mom and Dad were in a mandatory evacuation zone! Geez! Another worry! But we were fortunate that Hurricane George passed us by and recuperation could begin. I used the condo pool and Jacuzzi daily for some recovery.

After 2 ½ weeks with Mom and Dad, I needed to go home to get the medical care I needed from my regular doctors. Staying with Mom and Dad postponed my establishing a life for myself in California. I needed to get home and figure out what I wanted to do with the rest of my life.

My Leave of Absence was extended, as recovery wasn't as rapid as planned. When I returned to work, I needed to be able to run their pace, not the way I was operating before the Leave.

The total Leave was 7 weeks ... and I returned to a newly created job assignment.

Special Days with Mom and Dad ...

I wasn't able to physically spend Mom's birthday with her in Clearwater, but recognized it by gifts and flowers.

> Mom wrote the following in a thank you card afterwards, "Honey, I had to thank you for making my birthday the best ever! The charm with the birthstone and engraving is exquisite. I'm glad you let me put your (baby) ring and (baby) locket on the bracelet where I felt they belonged. (Another miracle that she never threw those out!) Some truly treasured memories united at last! (If there is a tear or two - forgive - ok?) We have so many "firsts" this year, but my birthday has always been important to me and to share that with you and Dad after all these years is a miracle! A dream come true! See you next week, we really miss you. Love You Baby, Mom"

We were able to enjoy Thanksgiving weekend together with Thanksgiving Day dinner at the country club.

For Christmas, including Dad's birthday on Christmas Eve, and several days afterwards, I was able to be with Mom and Dad, for more memorable times together.

Death of My Godmother ...

In early 1999, my godmother, Aunt Norm, had a stroke in Tucson, Arizona. Mom was executor of her Will including her Medical Power of Attorney, so had to be involved in final care decisions.

I offered to go to Tucson to assist Mom and Dad with things there. Neither of them was feeling very well. Mom had been getting shots in her knee; Dad had been scheduled for eye surgery, which was consequently postponed. Again, more health issues were on the horizon for them.

Aunt Norm was in a coma, but Mom told her I was on my way to see her. Interestingly, she held on until I arrived. She hadn't awakened from her coma until I was standing at her bedside next to Mom. When she saw us together, she smiled. That was really the first time I remember seeing her. She tried to talk with us, but couldn't. She held my hand and squeezed my fingers. I told her I was very happy to be reunited with my Mom and happy to know her as my godmother. She smiled at us and went back into her coma. The next day she passed away.

As Mom met with Aunt Norm's attorney, Mom and Dad were considering how to raise the funds needed for Aunt Norm's burial and attorney fees for her estate handling. Remember, this was the eccentric lady who took the sugar packets off the table when Mom and Dad would take her out to dinner, so they thought she was destitute! The attorney proceeded to shock Mom and Dad with the reality that my godmother died a multi-millionaire! Most was left to charity according to her Will and fortunately several organizations were helped by these funds.

There is a big lesson here, however, in living while you can. Instead of keeping new things in boxes in the closets, Aunt Norm should have used and enjoyed them. My great-grandmother's gorgeous Czechoslovakian crystal lamp was in two cardboard boxes under the kitchen sink! Aunt Norm used the Styrofoam bottoms from meat packages as plates, when she had lovely china and glassware available. She used old calendars as placemats, when new placemats were unopened, stored in the closet. Instead of living so frugally, she could have used some of her money to enjoy life more ... maybe go out to dinner or out with friends, have people in to visit her, go on trips, or be involved in other activities rather than living like a hermit.

Mom counseled me that Aunt Norm really had a problem going on with life after her husband died. (This was the husband Aunt Norm had Mom bury under the birdbath. It is hard to move on with this reminder in your front yard!) I think it's sad that she didn't use some of her money for grief counseling and try to move on with life.

It took a couple of trips to Tucson to help Mom and Dad get things cleared out of Aunt Norm's house. She had saved everything! She was apparently trying to inventory and organize all of her things in some manner when her stroke occurred.

This was another good lesson, this time in downsizing when one is able to face that task, rather than wait until it is too overwhelming. Mom and Dad had faced a similar crisis in their lives about downsizing after Dad's heart attack. The house they lived in was lovely, spacious, and positioned along the Inter-Coastal Waterway. But the upkeep was too great and Dad could no longer handle it. So, both agreed it was time to downsize; condominium living seemed to be the best alternative for them. They decided and acted on it while they both could.

Some Progress Being Made ...

With work commitments, my Clearwater visits weren't as frequent in 1999. But my driving need to see them so often was finally ebbing as well. I was really trying to make the most of each day and not wish my life away anxiously awaiting my next trip.

I came to the conclusion that I couldn't retire comfortably for several more years. So, I needed to do my best for my employer in the meantime. Work was becoming a priority again.

Also, any decision to sell my California property would not allow me to afford getting back into the California market at a future date, so I really needed to try making the bi-coastal arrangement work effectively. At this point, I thought maybe I'd just consider myself one of the "snowbirds" as they are called in Florida ... visiting in one state and living in another.

My need to journal started to lessen. I was much more at peace; felt I was living each day to the best that I could, where I could; problems were lessened; I was not so driven.

I made a quick trip to Clearwater the weekend just before my birthday.

> In a note Mom wrote afterwards, she said, "Honey: Always at this time of year, I used to gradually slide into a "Blue Funk" and come out of it about two days after your birthday. What changes your appearance on the scene has made! February is no longer dreaded! We are so lucky to have each other again! I love you this much! Mom LCA" (LCA means Love Conquers All).

Mom's sad times seemed to be fewer as were mine. Finally we were both making progress!

My next trip to see Mom and Dad was for Mother's Day 1999. We went to church together on Mother's Day, then out to dinner with Carol.

Dad was having a second cataract surgery and I was able to be there for it. Mom seemed relieved to have me there. A complication occurred during surgery; but with a subsequent doctor treatment, we thought Dad was on the mend.

Mom's knees were much improved.

So, I left both of them in improved conditions at the end of that visit.

Ohio Visit Finally Happens ...

In late May, we finally made the Ohio visit planned so long ago.

I met Mom, Dad, and Dad's niece, Marlene, and husband, Harry, at the Cincinnati Airport. Then, we went to Dad's sister's house to meet Aunt Marion. Meeting all of them, and the laughs we had together, made for some special and lasting memories.

Then, Mom, Dad and I drove to Cleveland to see my relatives. We had lunch with Aunt Phyl and her family. We didn't go into too many details of the past, just talked about various family stories. No one brought up the "infamous" letters, which made for a more pleasant visit!

For dinner, we met my Uncle Rich and his wife, Aunt Diane, and had a wonderful dinner together. Uncle Rich and I were very emotional at times, but enjoyed our visit.

He drove us over to an Assisted Care facility where my great-aunt was living, and we visited with her and two other aunts. We talked some about the past, with my emphasis being we can't recover or change it, so we need to move forward. I asked forgiveness for judging them on the basis of things I had been told when I was raised by my father and stepmother.

Mom got asked a few questions about what really happened between her and father. I listened to a few stories about money loaned to father that was never repaid and told them to get in line for all the money he owed me. That closed that discussion.

We had breakfast with my Uncle Rich and Aunt Diane before we left town the next day. He commented that lots of things have happened; but the opportunity that I have now with my new family, who obviously loves me a lot, is what counts going forward. He also emphasized that, while my father made some mistakes, don't ever doubt that he loved me. He urged me to go on now with the love God's given me from my Mom and step-dad and hopefully include the rest of the family when I can.

I know I couldn't have handled these meetings anytime sooner than we did. It was emotional enough for me ... and Mom ... even at this point. But I believe I did what God wanted me to do, asked forgiveness from those I was judging on the basis of past viewpoints of others, and did it when the time was right, with Mom and Dad as support. At least I could handle whatever topic arose and not be too defensive; and now it's time for the future! One day at a time and that day with the Lord!

June and July Visits to Clearwater ...

We enjoyed another Father's Day together. We enjoyed dinner out with Carol after church and played some Bingo when we returned home.

Dad's eye was still giving him problems and Mom's knee was still an issue from the accident repercussions.

Mom and I shared a love for reading, which was a good thing considering the recovery time needed from all of the health situations!

I prefer spy, detective, lawyer, or doctor books; on the other hand, Mom likes romantic, historic novels. When Mom finds a selection that combines some of the plots I like, she's happy to recommend it for me to read - provided it's not "too steamy!" Here I am 50+ years old and Mom's looking out for proper reading materials for her "kid!" I guess one never stops being a Mom no matter at what age the role becomes a reality!

I spent the remainder of the trip getting some furniture for my room, converting it more into an office as well as a bedroom, for working remotely more effectively when I came to visit.

> During a July visit and after a night of some "bear shenanigans," a note from Mom said: "Good Morning, Doll! When I see how much you are like me, it is almost scary, but oh so wonderful! It's also scary to realize we might not have even met! WOW! We are so lucky the Lord looked out for us. You are my miracle Baby! Love, Mom LCA"

Dad's Health Worsens ...

In August, on top of the continuing eye problems, Dad was losing his voice. His throat would be scratchy by the end of the day. He was generally feeling exhausted.

His health worsened in September. I could tell by Mom's call that she was at wit's end. Rather than being in California worrying about both of them, going to Mom and Dad's seemed like the best idea. Mom was immediately relieved I was coming the next day. I spent three weeks in Florida working remotely again.

Dad was hospitalized shortly after I arrived. After a week of tests, we learned the very sad news that he had an inoperable, malignant tumor of the esophagus.

Mom and Dad had agreed that each would make their own decision about their choice of continuing health care or foregoing treatment. It was very difficult to hear Dad announce that he wanted no further treatment. Ever since I met Dad, he'd consistently said, "Don't mourn for me when the time comes. I've had it all, lived a full life, and am ready to go!"

Of course, saying it and then watching it unfold are two very different scenarios. But he took a very courageous stand. He tried to encourage Mom to accept his decision, which she did support and respect, even though she wished it was different. It broke my heart when she told Dad, "I want to go too. I can't go on without you."

I'll never forget Dad's response to Mom's plea. Dad said, "We think and God does. All we can do is accept His decisions."

It would be hard enough to lose one of them. Selfishly, I felt sad that Mom didn't want to go on living without him when I was still in the picture. But I had to face the fact that her love for me was very different than her love for Dad. Mom was wrestling with the fact that she lost me for 45 years, and now must face another big loss … of the one who helped her make it out of the initial loss. Dad truly was her best friend and beloved life's partner.

Mom and Dad felt badly that I came back into their lives only to now have to face their health problems, after dealing with my stepmother's health issues. But God had a purpose in my coming back when I did and, if He thinks I can handle it, they are not to worry.

The doctors promised to keep Dad comfortable. While we would welcome a miracle cure, we had to prepare for his likely decline and help him conserve strength when possible, get him help when needed, and love him while we still had him. Hospice was there to assist and allow him to remain at home.

After Dad's diagnosis, we were to attend the wedding of Mom and Dad's godson, Andrew, to his bride, Michele, in Northern Florida. I drove Mom and Dad to the wedding festivities and Dad participated best as he could, considering his deteriorating health. He was so grateful to be able to attend that wedding and see Andrew and Michele so happy together. This was the last trip Dad made anywhere.

The doctors thought Dad's cancer was the slow and very painful kind, and because Dad's heart was so strong, they thought he would have a long six months battle. However, Dad and God knew otherwise.

As usual, Dad's first priority was Mom. He told me it was good that he would do some suffering at home, so Mom could see it and let him go easier. Since I spent much of his last five weeks with them, I know how he made all the plans for his funeral, and made sure he showed me the tasks I'd needed to do at Mom's after he couldn't do them anymore, like changing the air conditioner filter monthly. He "sold Mom" on his need to leave and challenged her to go on and live a full life with me.

He also charged me with taking care of Mom, which I would do willingly. He told me Mom was "a strong woman who comes from 'good stock' and we would probably have a good 10 years together" after he goes.

Dad helped Mom compose his obituary. One of the last requests he made of Carol and me was to have it imprinted on nice stationery, since he knew our plan was to hand it out at his funeral. He asked if he could read it one last time on the special stationery and was content after that.

Wow ... I hope I can be that strong when it's my turn to leave this world!

Dad died at home in early December, literally unable to eat during the last few weeks of his life. We got through his funeral with the support of family and friends. We even held a post-funeral luncheon at the country club featuring Dad's theme: "Don't Mourn for Me ... I've Had It All!" Carol helped me create a picture storybook to match the theme. It turned out to be healing for all of us.

Mom quickly scheduled her knee replacement surgery. She told the doctor that, since she had a broken heart now, she might as well put up with the surgery pain while she's at it. She had promised Dad she'd do the surgery as soon as possible, after having postponed it when he was diagnosed six weeks prior. Mom was determined to keep that promise.

> In a note Mom wrote to me the night before her surgery, she said, "Honey ... if something does happen tomorrow and I'm with Dad, please remember our 3 years - not the 45 that went before. I love you this much! Mom LCA"

That sure was a tough note to read! I hadn't even considered that possibility. But even in her grief for Dad, she was thinking of me with some encouragement, just in case. I was so relieved her surgery went well!

A Special Christmas ...

With Dad's birthday on Christmas Eve and this being the first Christmas without him, plus Mom's knee surgery recovery in process, I knew it was going to be a tough holiday season.

But leave it to that strong woman who I lovingly call "Mom." She booked a Christmas reception at a nearby beach hotel and a few day stay there for her, Carol, and me. Thirty-two friends attended the Christmas Eve reception in the hotel suite; and several joined us for Christmas Day dinner as well. We celebrated the holiday in a way that was healing, memorable, and would have made Dad proud.

The tears still flowed, especially when we returned to Cove Cay after the Christmas weekend. But lots of friends rallied to help Mom; I knew she was trying to be brave and busy.

She bravely faced the loss of Dad from a position of "NO REGRETS!" She said they had a wonderful life together. She always said she would spend as much time with him as she could, and when God took him, she knew she'd have to go on without him.

I was so relieved that I didn't have to deal with a negative attitude or self-pity, like I did with my stepmother. I couldn't express how grateful to God I was that Mom was so determined to go on with her life, and not reflect negatively on mine.

It was time for me to be working more in California. As soon as Mom's knee healed sufficiently, she planned to travel out to visit me.

We had an April cruise to the Riviera booked to look forward to. It was a combined Christmas and Mother's Day gift from me.

> Her thank you note to me after I returned to California said, "Honey, you really do have a "knack" for making me feel special. Everything was super, but best of all was our being together. I kind of feel like our years are like a diamond necklace, never losing the sparkle and lasting forever. I love you this much - Mom"

"Forever" was the operative word. We were reminded of it again, seeing a glimpse of it through the loss of Dad. We knew we'd see him again when we get to Heaven.

What's Next? ...
"We think and God does," Dad had said.

Several life-changing events occurred over the past few years and we must accept the results and press on. For now, God chose Mom and I to continue in our journey together.

Whatever tomorrow brings, Mom and I will face it together ... with God's help.

We're not so focused on what was stolen from us; we're now more focused on what we have.

Chapter 6

MOVING ON

*"Remember not the former things, neither consider
the things of old. Behold, I will do a new thing."*
Isaiah 43: 18-19a

Mom was recovering well from her knee surgery, through sheer determination and pool therapy, to get back on her feet again.

Naturally, she was heavy-hearted at times due to losing Dad. But she didn't allow herself to mourn or pity for long. She got busy and kept busy!

She still enjoyed the Cove Cay lifestyle and was involved there with people and projects. Friends and family rallied to help her as needed. There was no way Carol, Carl, or I would allow Mom to be alone or inactive for long. But Mom was a very strong person and didn't require our nudging very often.

I believe the depth of Mom's hurt was so devastating, because of our missing 45 years, that she was determined to handle the grief of Dad's passing quicker than expected. She knew Dad was no longer hurting, that there wasn't anything else that could have been done to help him. She knew they did all they could together for as long as they had each other and knew that she'd see him again in Heaven one day. Dad had asked her to go on without him and make a new life with me. She promised him she would and was going to keep that promise.

She didn't let Dad's passing negatively affect her life or mine. It doesn't mean she didn't cry, have times of regret, and miss him deeply. After all, he was her best friend. But she didn't let those times consume her.

When Mom wanted my company, and to ease her being alone whenever that feeling overwhelmed her, she had an open invitation to come visit me and stay as long as she wanted. She loved to travel, so welcomed the opportunity. The fear of flying was Dad's, after his years of traveling for his work; Mom wasn't fearful, but just went along with Dad's preference, so he didn't have to stay home by himself. Now that she was free to travel, she was back to looking forward to those times. She could rarely sleep the night before a trip, and not so well a whole week prior, due to excitement for wherever the destination was.

Mom wanted to explore doing other things in her life, and urged me to have my own life, my own friends, and my own space. So, for now, it was good for us to live in two different locations.

I would still visit her once a month, but focused more on work in California. Daily cards and phone calls continued to be our mainstays when she was on one Coast and me on the other. Our love continued to grow each day.

Mom's "Grandkid" Cricket ...

For February, Mom scheduled a trip to visit and wanted to stay with me, which presented a few obstacles to overcome. I didn't want her staying in a motel, but was concerned about her allergy to dogs. But Mom felt I'd given up enough in my life and didn't want to see me give up Cricket, if it could be helped.

Besides, she liked dogs and wanted to enjoy one in her lifetime, if possible. Since Cove Cay doesn't allow pets, I gave Mom a battery-operated robot dog that she named "Sparky." For sure, he was allergy-free, but naturally didn't have the same appeal as a real one.

Mom offered to get re-tested for her dog allergy and learned she was primarily allergic to cats, not so much to dogs. The doctor prescribed some allergy medicine to allow her to be around Cricket, if she did have any problems during the visit.

Meanwhile, I had enough time to "de-dog" the house before her arrival. A thorough house cleaning, including rugs and draperies, and setting up portable air filter units throughout the house, all helped my allergies too!

Now, I just had to make sure Cricket could expand her horizon to include Mom … or I should say "Grandma." Needless to say, it was easier to "de-dog" the house than to get this stubborn, one-person, Chow dog to allow another person to quickly get close to her! Mom said she, "worked harder to win over Cricket than she did her second husband!" But love and perseverance won out - along with lots of steak bones and baked chicken smuggled in her carry-on luggage when coming to see us!

Cricket could be very accommodating with the right bribe! Mom would occasionally go to the pet store … but stood at the door of the shop and asked the clerk to find her a toy for her "grandkid." She was unable to go in herself, due to the serious cat and bird allergies she did have. The toy would come with the steak bone or chicken bribe and gained Mom even faster acceptance! One of Cricket's favorite toys was a blue and white stingray from Florida … from Grandma!

Eventually, Mom and Cricket became fast friends … with Mom even sending Cricket cards in the mail to give messages to "Cricket's Mom" from "Grandma!" The bear "grandkids" even got involved and sent Cricket cards too! More examples of Mom's and my unique senses of humor - and mutual enjoyment!

The winning moment, however, was when Cricket realized "Grandma" could drive the car and take Cricket for rides when she visited! Of course, I was relegated to the back seat, and Cricket generally sat in the front passenger seat if Grandma drove. She became known as the "Cadillac Queen" … Cricket, that is! You may be wondering who ran my household and you're getting a clear glimpse of that by this insight!

We actually had to spell the word R-I-D-E … just in case Cricket wasn't to be invited. "NO" was not an acceptable alternative when we appeared to be going for a R-I-D-E somewhere! W-A-L-K was another four-letter word spelled around my house. One day I was talking with Mom and actually asked, "Do we need any M-I-L-K from the store?" while thinking about taking Cricket with me to the store. Momentarily, I got confused about which words we had to spell!

Mom tried to tell me that Cricket could work the car's electric windows … to which I said, "Sure, Mom, yah." I knew she thought Cricket was the smartest dog she'd ever known, but this was a little extreme! Then, when I had Cricket in the front passenger seat one day on a ride, all of a sudden Cricket was looking at me very indignantly with her body pushed up against the dashboard and her nose almost pressed to the front window! I thought, "How did that happen?!" I pulled over and fixed the seat before we could take off again. Sure enough, I saw Cricket lean her front right elbow on the door arm rest, like she saw me doing, and all of a sudden the seat started easing forward again ... her elbow was on the electric seat button! Made for interesting errand rides!

Mom's Visit to California ...

During Mom's February visit, we had our 3rd year Reunion Anniversary and enjoyed a backyard party with friends to help us celebrate. She stayed long enough for us to make an enjoyable trip to San Diego to celebrate my birthday.

When it was time for her Florida return, I was ill ... but Mom made some of her "guaranteed-to-cure-you" homemade beef vegetable soup before she left, to aid in a speedier recovery. That and numerous get-well cards made for a complete recovery!

Expanding Clearwater Activities ...

Mom started getting busy helping others at Cove Cay. If any friends needed transportation, Mom was there with "Big Red II" offering to assist. She gladly took them to doctor appointments, errands, shopping, and church. She enjoyed lunches and dinners out with friends as well.

On Wednesday mornings, Mom became active in a Clearwater Christian organization called "The Breakfast Club," at the invitation of some Cove Cay friends. This offered her some Christian fellowship during the week, not just on Sundays. She participated in their occasional group trips that were scheduled within the U.S. or abroad.

Mom started feeling unhappy at her Presbyterian church and wondered what to do about it. She told me she would sit in church and could picture Dad coming in and sitting next to her like he used to. Having that mind-picture repeatedly made her sad. Besides that, the new minister hadn't effectively ministered to her during Dad's illness and death. So, she didn't feel tied to that church any longer.

I told her "God doesn't want you to be unhappy in His House ... so it might be God's way of moving you along to a different church." She accepted that thought and began exploring other possibilities, visiting other churches in the Clearwater area.

She learned when she came to visit me why I enjoyed the Baptist church I was attending, and looked forward to attending there whenever she'd come to see me. Little did she know then that God had plans for her in that church in the not-too-distant future.

Other Trips Together ...

In April, Mom and I took our two-week Mediterranean Cruise, starting in Rome and ending in Barcelona. We flew over to Europe from New York.

Before we left New York though, we went to see the Statue of Liberty. I took pictures on Ellis Island of my relatives' names, the Ruzicka's from Czechoslovakia, carved into the memorial among those who registered there during their immigration to the United States. That was a very special memory.

Mom loved Rome the most ... having been there with Dad many years prior. With him, she had thrown a coin into the Trevi Fountain, which signified good luck and promise of a return visit someday. I was able to share her return visit with her.

Our photo album provides good memories of the places we visited. Mom's favorite travel picture of me is when we first boarded the ship. Mom looked very lovely, well rested, enjoying herself immensely, and excited to be getting on board. I, on the other hand, looked like I didn't know which way it was to the ship! I was very tired from getting ready for the vacation, was hauling too much luggage for both of us, and looked like I hadn't combed my hair in several days! When I saw the proof of that ship photo, I said, "We sure don't want that picture as a memory!"

Mom said quickly, "Oh yes, I do!" She laughed about that all the time, reflecting back to this trip! After I recuperated, I too could see the humor!

In May, we enjoyed Mother's Day together. Carol joined us for dinner in Tampa. Then, Mom and I traveled together out to California for a long weekend at Pismo Beach. She stayed several days extra with Cricket and me before returning to Cove Cay.

I spent Father's Day weekend in Clearwater with Mom. I knew that would be a hard day for both of us. Together we overcame any sadness.

Mom joined the "computer age" that trip. I had the computer set up in my Cove Cay bedroom and showed Mom how to sign on and email me. This became our twice-daily communication method … plus phone calls when we needed to hear each other's voices.

She actually named her computer, "Al," short for Alba, her mother's name. Mom said her mother often gave her a hard time just like Mom felt the computer did!

I got into the routine of emailing Mom each night before I'd go to bed, so I'd say, "Let's go tell Grandma goodnight!" And guess who would quickly head out to the study ahead of me and lay by my feet until I was done? Yes, Cricket knew who Grandma was! When I didn't head there fast enough at night, Cricket would start whining. I'd look at her wondering what was wrong. Then, she'd head out to the study and I figured out, it was "time to talk with Grandma!"

When Mom would leave me a voice message, Cricket would bark when she'd hear Grandma's voice! Guess she was trying to tell her to get to California so she could have a R-I-D-E again!

In September, Mom came to California. We took some vacation time for a trip to Morro Bay in Central California. Then, she was able to join me on a work outing as my guest at our Management Appreciation Weekend in Napa Valley, in Northern California. I was proud to have her with me and she was happy to meet my colleagues!

Surprise 75th Birthday Party! …

Carol and I surprised Mom with her 75th birthday party at Cove Cay in November 2000. It is a challenge to plan a surprise party from across the country! So, Carol did much of the local work coordinating party plans and was happy to help with all of that.

I called Mom from California to ask her to reserve her birthday afternoon for a dinner between Carl and family, Carol, and myself. I suggested we have lunch at the Country Club, as it was a central location between Carl's and Carol's, so convenient for all to meet there. Little did I realize, on that day of the week, the only things the Club normally served were hamburgers and hot dogs! I'm sure Mom thought I was operating under a very restrained budget or was just cheap! But she didn't say anything except, "Sure, that's great!" True to her style, she wasn't going to embarrass me and went along with my suggestion.

We got it all together, had a terrific menu, about 70 people participated, and the program was successful. Best of all, Mom was actually surprised at her Surprise 75th Birthday Party!

> In a thank you card afterwards, she wrote, "You have packed so many blessings into the last four years! It would take rolls of paper to mark them down. But I don't have to keep track - God will! You have been there for me when I ask and even more important, when I don't ask, you anticipate. You are my kid and I love you this much and forever. Thank you again for that wonderful well planned party – Mom"

Christmas Plans ...

December 2000 marked the anniversary of Dad's death, and his Christmas Eve birthday, so I knew this year's Christmas season would be difficult to get through. I suggested to Mom we go on a Christmas Cruise - and she was all for it. We booked a one-week Caribbean Cruise for a relaxing getaway.

The cruise proved memorable for several reasons, starting with missing the ship's first port! It seemed the cruise line's airline had a fleet of only one plane, and that plane from Miami to Aruba had engine problems.

Many passengers were upset and insisted we be able to get on board. They were being so rude and illogical, I finally yelled at them, "Are you crazy? You want to get on a plane with engine problems?!" The cruise line finally put us up at a hotel for the night and would fly us to St. Thomas to rendezvous with the ship.

That was provided we lived to get to that flight!

It was Christmas Day and the bus driver must have been "in training." She was so bad at driving the bus that she tried exiting the entrance of the parking area, which would have blown out the tires if the guard standing in the pouring rain didn't frantically re-direct her. Then, she backed up into a palm tree trying to turn the bus around! While heading out toward the exit, she literally hit four different cars before successfully leaving the parking lot. She never even stopped to leave a note about any of the accidents!

No one on the bus dared to say anything; we were eyes front! Mom and I didn't dare look at each other or we would have busted out laughing ... it was so ludicrous!

The driver was obviously in the Christmas spirit, as she was playing Christmas music and humming along the whole trip to the airport, having a great time!

Everyone applauded when we arrived at the airport, and the driver thanked us profusely thinking we enjoyed the ride! At least everyone was done complaining about missing the first flight and port; they were just happy to be alive to get to the next port!

A delightful memory we had was being served Christmas Day brunch on our St. Thomas hotel patio overlooking the lovely bay view ... once we finally arrived at that port!

That's where we boarded the ship the day after Christmas - only to learn that hundreds of kids who were off school were cruising with their parents! This was another eye-opener!

Mom might have had a little anger issue to deal with herself when, one time too many, she got on the ship's elevator and the kids had pushed every deck, not planning to get off at any one of them! One of the kids had a cup of hot chocolate in his hand and one rambunctious youngster too many was on board the elevator. Mom looked sternly at that rowdy child and said, "You will be careful not to spill that beverage on me, young man, correct?!" That seemed to settle the kids down, who were operating totally unsupervised on board this elevator ride!

One thing we learned: it is not a good season for "seasoned" people with "patience issues" to travel! But we made it through this tough anniversary ... together!

2001 Brings Big Changes ...

Right after New Year's, God started talking with Mom about what she was still doing in Florida. Mom said she'd be reading her Bible or praying, and His voice would say to her, "You didn't know where Janet was for 45 years, but you know now. Why are you still in Florida?"

Mom would argue, "Florida is my home and has been for all these years."

"You should be out in California helping Janet," God would respond.

She tried again, "But I am helping people here ... taking them to doctor appointments; besides, Janet should have her own life." God didn't let her win that argument either.

She tried to ignore the issue for a long time. But the pushback would come again and God wouldn't leave her alone. She never mentioned this to me at this point.

Mom had some big reservations before she could respond positively to God on this issue. Consider that if she lived with me in California, she would be living in my father and stepmother's house, the place I had been abused. She couldn't stand that thought. She was also concerned about my living my own life. She knew I was just starting to enjoy living by myself, and didn't believe it was a good idea for her to move in with me.

When Mom visited me in February, she casually inquired what I was going to do when I retired. I said, "I hadn't thought about it because it's still a few years away. But I would want to be near you."

"I thought you didn't like Florida and wouldn't want to move there," Mom responded.

"That's true," I said, "the humidity bothers me too much. But I would want to be near to you. So, if you're in Florida, I need to go there and find a way to tolerate it."

The next statements shocked me. She said, "Then, I think we should start looking for a place near you I can rent. I've been looking in the paper for the past few days and wanted you to show me some of the listings."

"Are you talking about moving out here?!" I questioned.

Because of my response, Mom thought I didn't want her to move here and responded, "I know if something happens to my health, you'd want me near you. So, while I still have a few good years left, why shouldn't I come out and help you? If I can run errands for some elderly ladies in Clearwater, I can do it for you and want to!"

I don't know why she didn't realize her suggestion was a total shock to me! It came out of left field!! But I was actually thrilled for her to be considering that! So, I assured her, "That was a terrific idea! You just surprised me by even suggesting it! Last time we discussed the possibility of your moving here, you said emphatically you weren't ready for that."

But she was more than ready now. Just like me, once it's decided, no turning back and let's get on with it!

Certainly I'd help her find a rental place, but pursued, "Why rent a place? Why don't you live with me? There's plenty of room!"

She insisted she would rather rent and let me preserve my freedom and independence. So, I didn't object any more about that right now. I just started thinking about where would be the best places to rent. We got started on that the next day and found a place she'd like that was only about 15 minutes drive from my house.

By the time Mom went back to Florida, we had compiled some TO DO Lists for her, so the overall move wouldn't become too overwhelming. She knew with work I wouldn't be able to assist in-person. But I knew she was a very capable lady and I trusted she'd get it all organized.

She immediately got her condo ready to put on the market! She had downsizing to do and a few repairs to handle; she had to find a realtor and execute paperwork to list the unit; and began notifying friends and neighbors that she was moving to California. All knew why and weren't surprised; they were just very sad because they would miss Mom very much. Now they knew how I felt each time my visits with her ended!

So, at 75 years old, Mom orchestrated her move to California! Carl offered to drive "Big Red II" out to California. Mom arranged for a mover; began giving away whatever she wasn't taking with her; started packing things that could be shipped ahead. She was saying good-bye to an area she had lived in for over 40 years. This was not an easy task. It could only be done out of love … for me, and, of course, because God wasn't giving her a moment's peace!

Mom's condo sold in March … to close in May.

I flew to Clearwater in mid-April, to help Mom with final move decisions and preparations.

In May, Mom was flying to California to live there! Her furniture was in route … so was Carl with "Big Red II." Cricket was delighted that "Grandma" was going to be around more to take her for R-I-D-E-s! I was ecstatic! What a welcome, yet unexpected, turn of events!

Mother's Day 2001 …

We spent Mother's Day together in California.

I had entered Mom in a "Mother's Day" contest offered by a local radio station. Mom didn't win the contest … but she'd always be a WINNER to me! I had submitted the following entry and gave it to her as a Mother's Day gift:

"One-in-a-Million" Mom

After 45 years of being separated, my Mom's greeting was:

"Hi Sweetheart, how are you?"

I'd found Mom alive and willing to talk, following a lifetime of
believing I was unwanted.

Between tears and fears, I ventured,
"Why would a mother not want her child?"

Shockingly, I learned that my father kidnapped me at five
years old and fled to California. Searches were unsuccessful …
Mom had lost her only child.

Finally, she forged a new life with a wonderful man
(eventually, my dear step-dad).

In February 1997, we reunited by phone, then met two weeks
later. Doubts and hurts gradually gave way to Mom's gift of
unconditional love!

Nothing recovers lost years. Nothing erases grief of past
Mother's Days. Sadly, an abusive upbringing repressed my
memories of Mom. But we finally agree: the past is just that.
We only have NOW!

So, Mom is bravely relocating cross-country … to help me while
her health permits … to be nearer for each moment God allows.

It's not easy to call someone "Mom" after 45 years … to
understand unconditional love if you never felt it … to
"go public" with this story … unless you have …
my "One-in-a-Million" Mom!

Happy Mother's Day, 2001
Love ALWAYS,
J'Gay

I was actually worried Mom would be upset that I submitted this contest
entry without her permission. My stepmother would have been furious or
made fun of me for doing something like this. But not my Mom! She felt
honored, as I'd hoped she would.

To top it all off, my church, Puente Hill Baptist, named Mom the "2001
Mother of the Year." They recognized Mom's story and testimony as special.

They knew of her support for me and now were witnesses of her sacrifice to move cross-country at 75 years old as a sign of her unconditional love for me. She was presented with a Thomas Kinkade lighted, ceramic church in memory of this honor.

This special Mother's Day recognition was a "once-in-a-lifetime" opportunity for Mom, after so many years of dreading this day. I don't remember if she cried, but I did … tears of joy about us being together!

More Mom News …

Mom started attending Puente Hills Baptist Church regularly as soon as she moved to California. She loved the music and preaching. She especially liked studying the Bible, like never before in her Presbyterian background.

Before the end of the year, and unbeknownst to me, she had inquired of Pastor Trisler about how to join the church. Since she was already a born-again Christian, he told her she would just have to be baptized by immersion. She had only been baptized by sprinkling, as a child in her Presbyterian church, and that was not enough according to the Baptist's Bible-based beliefs. Mom wanted to be baptized as required in the Baptist church and did so at 76 years old - proving one is never too old! With that act, and her personal testimony, Mom became a member of Puente Hills Baptist Church.

We were able to worship and serve the Lord together there over the next few years. What a great joy that was!

We went on a two-week Cruise to the Northern Capitals of Europe to celebrate her re-location and Mother's Day. We were starting a new chapter in our lives!

On the ship's elevator one day, I questioned Mom about whether what I planned to wear to the formal dinner was appropriate. She said, "I'm sure it will be fine. Besides, what do you care? You're never going to see these people again!"

Overhearing this conversation, the lady next to us decided to adopt that great philosophy to relieve future stress on these types of situations! I've used it frequently and smile each time thinking of Mom's simple, but insightful, conclusion!

Mom only lived in the rental property for about six months, and was staying overnight at my house about 80% of the time! I would find good excuses for her to spend the night: too late for her to drive back by herself or an errand to run from my house first thing in the morning. I really didn't want her to leave to go to her rental place.

Finally, she agreed that living in two close locations was not the wisest alternative. She knew we got along well, and I was very happy having her staying with me. She agreed to move into the house with me but only if she could share ½ of the expenses. That worked out well for both of us … actually, for all three of us; Cricket was as happy for the extra attention as I was!!

Big Changes at Work …

In April 2001, our division went through an unexpected, huge layoff. My team and our project were part of those budget cuts. I had been temporarily reassigned to another project that would not continue past December 31, 2001. I was offered the opportunity to early retire at that point after 28 years with the company.

When you pray that you'd like to be as happy at work as you are off work and weekends, sometimes God's answer is, "Okay, work somewhere else." I just needed to accept the news and move on … where, I wasn't sure.

On September 14, at the chiropractor's, in traction no less, the Lord told me, "When you're ready to be happier, just let Me know." Wow! I told God I was ready and listening to where He wanted me to go next.

It didn't take long to find out what God had planned to make me happier.

On September 21, I learned about an opportunity with a non-profit organization, with which I had been affiliated through my company for several years. The position of President would be available as of January 1, 2002. I accepted that position when offered by the organization's Board of Directors.

In mid-December, the company from which I was early retiring gave me a farewell reception. Some friends and family came to a retirement party at my house, as this career came to an end. Mom was able to participate in both events, which was another advantage of her closer proximity!

Immediately, work began with my exciting new assignment for the non-profit organization. Mom was there to support this transition as well as being willing to work as the "unpaid staff" of this organization! Planning and executing payroll tax industry conferences was a primary objective of this organization. So, Mom and I had great times planning the conferences, one in Spring 2002 in Washington, D.C, another in Fall 2002 in Palm Springs, California.

Mom would be the answer person at the conference's reception desk, helping direct traffic and field questions. She knew we were on a tight budget. One time someone from another conference walked by our refreshment display and Mom saw him palm a soft drink from our refreshment table! If Mom could have vaulted the reception desk she was behind, that man could have been injured, I'm sure! She was so upset that someone would take one of our $2 soft drinks from our display without even asking or offering to pay for it!

Needless to say, we learned lots from working these conferences together. Both events were declared successful and we were feeling encouraged about the results and some growth we were seeing in the organization!

Some Personal Insights ...

Mom was available and happy to run errands and keep the house running smoothly, while I worked from home for this non-profit organization.

Mom loved to cook, so fixing good meals was a joy for her - and she made it look so easy! My specialties were cold cereal or cheese quesadillas! Cricket was thrilled that Grandma loved to cook things like Prime Rib or chicken - and neither of us was wanting for good food or plenty of it with Mom around!

Daily trips to the Post Office were required for the business and Mom made these trips with her sidekick, Cricket! If she went at the noon hour, Cricket "serenaded" her with barking to the church bells that rang across the street from the Post Office. I rode with them occasionally and you actually had to hold your fingers over your ears, Cricket's barking was so loud in the closed up car! Mom just laughed and seemed to love it!

Another errand Mom ran for me was to the vet's office to pick up Cricket's prescription - with Cricket as her passenger. She said Cricket started crying or "howling sadly" as soon as she got near the building. While Mom went in to pick up the prescription, she could hear Cricket from the parking lot all the way into the building!

One customer said, "Your dog isn't very happy about having an appointment today!"

Mom said, "Funny thing, she isn't even getting out of the car today! She just came along for the ride! She just doesn't even want to be in the vet's neighborhood!"

Cricket was so afraid of the vet that I would call them to ask if they could give Cricket what I called a "drive-by shooting" for periodic shots she required. I would offer to hold Cricket in my arms in the car; then, the vet assistant would reach into the car with the syringe and give Cricket her shot of the medicine. Being a long time customer, they were happy to accommodate that request, which simplified their work and my stress in handling my testy and reluctant 80-pound Chow!

When the Santa Ana winds blew in Southern California, the wind really howled. It would cause the doors to whistle and the chimney to make funny noises, and Cricket would get scared. One night I was sitting on the floor in the hallway, comforting Cricket due to the howling winds … and because the roof had blown loose and was flapping in the wind!

The sound of the roof flapping made so much noise, I wasn't able to sleep.

Mom got up for a restroom break and saw me sitting with Cricket. She commented, "Hi Sweetheart, what's going on?"

"The wind is scaring Cricket and the roof is blowing off," I replied.

"Oh, that's nice," Mom said and went back to bed!

I thought, "Boy, she really doesn't rattle easily, does she!" But that was the moment I learned she actually doesn't wake up once she's asleep until she's ready to get up in the morning! She was sort of sleepwalking to the bathroom!

The next day I mentioned the conversation we had, and Mom asked, "What conversation?" That was an important lesson for me to learn: be careful what I discussed with her in the middle of the night!

Mom loved to have Christmas decorations displayed and we had many boxes of them in the garage. She didn't want me on a ladder anymore putting up the lights; so, she would hire someone to do the job each Christmas season. When she paid for these services the first year, she jokingly said, "Okay, Janet Gayle, you have twelve months to find someone to date who can put up those lights for you next year!"

That got to be a private joke, whenever I'd see someone who looked attractive to me. She'd say, "He looks like he could hang lights!"

One time I was in line at the airport talking with this nice looking gentleman who was a magazine publisher from New York. Mom was sitting over by the windows, rather than standing in the ticket line with me. As I'm trying to pay attention to what this man is saying to me, I see movement to my right. I tried not to be obvious as I looked, but there's Mom with her arms stretched upright and apart, waving them back and forth, mouthing the words, "Can he hang Christmas lights?" How do you keep a straight face with this going on?! She was really a character and knew how to make me laugh!

5th Year Reunion Anniversary …
February 9, 2002 was our 5th year Reunion Anniversary.

> In my card to Mom, I wrote: "What a tremendous new life I've been given in finding you!! How blessed I feel as I consider how special and different life is for me now! Every day is brighter, better, and more exciting with you in my life. Your love makes me feel very special, safe, and basically WONDERFUL!
>
> I pray the Lord will allow us many more days together, memories to share, and times to enjoy! The laughter in my life is a great gift - much because of you!
>
> My love for you is greater than I ever could have imagined or hoped for. I love you more than THIS MUCH!
>
> J'Gay

Here we were working together and living together; we had done much traveling together; and we were enjoying each day together! We had made positive progress in our relationship far beyond what I could ever have imagined!

Big Changes at Home …
We went through a total remodel of my house in mid-2002! Like a garage sale, a house remodel should be experienced once in life … but only once! Yikes! It was total upheaval!

After 40 years, the house needed some repairs and updating. Mom recommended, rather than try to do that one room at a time, I should consider doing all I wanted to the house in a total remodel and refinance the house just once. That was a great idea and sounded logical! Little did I know what we were in for!

As the repairs got started, it became apparent some repairs were very significant and just in time! I thought one of the plastic wall plugs needed to be replaced, only to learn the electrical cables were disintegrated within the walls! All of the electrical cables needed replacing, which required holes to be punched in most of the walls in every room of the house! I used to think the movie, *"The Money Pit,"* was one of the funniest I had ever seen - until I was actually living a similar experience!

I had two bathrooms when this project started. My request was to keep one functional at all times. When I noticed both commodes out on the backyard patio slab, I knew my expectations were different from reality! The way the re-modelers chose to work this part of the project, Mom and I would have to trek up to McDonald's at the corner to use their facility for a few weeks until at least one of the bathrooms was functional again!

It was very challenging to be talking with prospective conference attendees from my home office, while all the pounding was going on or Cricket was barking at the workmen! Mom and Cricket had to sit in my one-room home office with me and all of our worldly goods, while the rest of the 7 rooms of the house were in total disarray in various stages of repair. They never seemed to finish one room before terrorizing another!

Yet, Mom never complained! Actually, I believe she was so happy the house was taking on a new look and becoming "ours," instead of "father's," she would have put up with living in a tent in the backyard to see this remodel accomplished!

Somehow we all persevered for the four months it took ... and the transformation of our 40-year old house was remarkable!

More Life Changes to Accept ...

A shocking call came into my home office in May 2003. It made me aware of some major, unpaid debts of this non-profit organization; these would prevent the organization from staying in business. These debts were incurred by the previous President and undisclosed at the time I assumed the responsibility. We fought it valiantly for a few months. But in the end, it was my first, and hopefully last, experience with "corporate" bankruptcy!

By July 2003, I was on unemployment, and very grateful for Mom sharing the household expenses with me! My next occupation was unknown at this point. But Mom was there to support me through it all.

God had told Mom to move out to California and help me; it was now apparent to us what He knew was going to unfold!

I started getting anxious about what my next career move needed to be. God apparently knew I needed to be slowed down to stay in synch with His timetable! The way He chose to do that was a painful but memorable way.

My two nieces were visiting Southern California in June 2003. Last Christmas they had asked Mom if she would be their "Grandma," to which she naturally said "Yes!" So, Grandma and Aunt Janet had enjoyed making some good memories with them by taking them to the Queen Mary and Catalina Island.

The last day they were visiting our area, I went to pick them up at their other aunt's house. My 1996 Cadillac was in their aunt's driveway as I loaded the trunk with their luggage, in order to take them to the airport after we visited a farm along the way.

I had set the emergency brake to safely load the trunk because the car was parked on an inclined driveway. But when I got back into the car, the emergency brake wouldn't release.

The Cadillac Manual's diagram showed a release mechanism under the dashboard when the brake was stuck like mine. My oldest niece was holding the Manual so I could see the picture, as I got out of the car and crouched down by the driver's seat. As I pulled the release, the entire car released … not just the emergency brake, and the car started rolling down the driveway. It knocked me down hard and started dragging me under the tires of the car. I only had a second to pray, "Help me, God!" I pushed away with my hands on the driveway, just as the car rolled over my toes, right rib cage, and right hand. The car door had me trapped and started dragging me down the driveway laid out on my back.

All of a sudden, where the driveway meets the sidewalk was just enough difference in elevation to release me from being pinned down and dragged further by the door. As the car kept rolling backwards down the cul-de-sac, with my nieces inside, I jumped up to go after them and thought, "I must be okay if I can stand up!" So, I ran after the rolling car. It hit the curb in back of it and rolled up on the neighbor's lawn, which stopped the roll. By then, my nieces were hysterical, crying and worrying about me!

I jumped into the car and said, "I think we need to go back to Grandma's and not to the farm right now." I asked my oldest niece to call Grandma and let her know we were on our way home. I took the phone and explained that the car had run over me. Mom didn't quite comprehend the severity of what I was saying and just replied, "Okay." I thought she was taking it very calmly, like the roof blowing off, not realizing she didn't fully understand what I was hurriedly explaining!

I was starting to hurt and have trouble catching my breath, now that the adrenaline was wearing off. My main goal was to get us back to the house as Mom didn't really know the area we were in, and wouldn't be able to locate us if I pulled off into a hospital along the way. Besides I was trying not to upset my nieces - a little late for that, in hindsight!

When we got home, I asked the girls to get Grandma for me. When Mom came out I said,

"Maybe you could help me to the passenger seat and you could drive me to the hospital, so I could get checked out."

Wisely Mom said, "Maybe I can call you an ambulance right now!" I guess I didn't look so good.

The emergency personnel said I was lucky to be alive ... as most of these types of accidents end in death or very severe injuries. I only had two broken ribs and lots of bruising, road rash, and pain. My right hand was spared any broken bones thanks to the two gold rings I was wearing; they kept the tire from squishing my three fingers that were run over! I was able to leave the hospital on my own later that afternoon.

Meanwhile, Mom took charge and rented a limousine to get the girls to the airport timely, while I was still in the Emergency Room. She came back for me after they were safely on their flight. Later, besides the fun at the Queen Mary and Catalina Island, the girls would be grateful for their memory of the "AWESOME Limo ride!" A good memory with Grandma following a harrowing experience with Aunt Janet!

It was truly a miracle I had survived! It would also be about six weeks, however, before I could maneuver without pain again. That's how God told me to, "Sit still and ... be anxious for nothing!" I finally "got the message" that it wasn't my season to look for work!

I had debated about writing the book about Mom's and my reunion story while I was unemployed and recuperating. So, I asked God about it. On June 23, He told me, "If you don't write it, Jan, who will?"

That sounded like I was supposed to get started on it. But I quickly learned

I was unable to concentrate following the accident and I couldn't sit at the computer for any length of time. I concluded: while I was supposed to write it, now wasn't the time.

This allowed for several other things to happen:

Mom proceeded to have her second knee replacement in August 2003. It was a rougher surgery than the first one; recovery slower than expected. I was Mom's "nurse."

I did pool therapy along with Mom to improve from the car accident residuals; my left leg and knee were both causing me some problems.

My left hand operation was in October 2003, to remove a painful arthritic joint. Mom was my "nurse." I knew she felt bad about missing other surgeries in my life; but I hoped God wasn't going to give her too much experience in this area other than this hand surgery!

An industry colleague, Fran, called me and invited me to a "Buccaneers" football game during the Thanksgiving weekend, while Mom and I were scheduled to be in Florida visiting Carol. My friend wanted to talk with me about a possible job opportunity with her company now that my "two-year non-compete" agreement had ended with the company from which I had early retired! (God's timing, not mine ... ah-ha! That's why I was supposed to slow down!).

Mom and I were able to do a lot of church work during the last few months of 2003. If I had been working, we couldn't have spent time together on these projects for the Lord.

Thanksgiving Interview and Subsequent Plans ...

We enjoyed the Thanksgiving holiday in Jupiter, Florida, visiting with Carol.

Then, we returned to the Tampa area, so I could attend the Buccaneers' game with Fran. She was telling me about her company, their job opportunities, and doing an interview - all in between the game plays!

The opportunity sounded interesting, and I accepted Fran's invitation to interview in Dallas within the next few weeks. I got the impression that there would be a job for me, it just depended on where I would best fit. That got me even more enthused about the opportunity. It sounded like a serious offer to come.

I asked Mom what she thought about moving to Texas if I accepted a job with Fran's company. Mom didn't even take 30 seconds before she said, "Well, I've never been to Texas, so let's go!"

Talk about good support ... I couldn't have asked for a better "cheerleader" in my corner, along with her "Mama Bear" role in my life! If it was good for me, Mom wanted it to happen. Her deepest desire, after we reunited, was for me never to be hurt again. I knew that probably was too optimistic of a position to take ... but she really did her best to make sure it was the case.

So, I booked a three-day trip to Dallas for Mom and me during the second week of December. While there I wanted to look around and see if there was a house for us that we both liked, in case the interview went well.

I interviewed with several executives. I liked what I saw and heard that first day. Fran introduced me to her realtor, Trish.

On the second day, Mom and I toured around the areas with Trish, looking at a several homes. I wasn't happy with what we saw. There was no way we were going to take on another home that needed remodeling! So, I changed some of the search criteria for Trish and asked her to meet us again on the third day with any other prospects.

Meanwhile, I prayed that night for the Lord to show us a place we'd like in our price range, if this was the right job opportunity for me to take on next. If it wasn't meant to be, I would know because we wouldn't be able to find a home we liked.

On day three, Trish picked us up at the agreed upon time. My first question to her was, "Well, did you find my dream home?"

Confidently, she said, "Yes, I believe I did!"

"You did??" I questioned unbelievingly. I thought maybe she was kidding, 'Doubting Thomas' that I was!

"You let me know what you think," Trish said, as we drove off to Farmers Branch, Texas.

When we entered the housing complex, I thought I was in a storybook land! It was a gorgeous neighborhood. I thought surely she was just driving down this road to get to the neighborhood where the house would actually be. Nope! She stopped in front of this beautiful brick house in this complex and said, "This is it."

Remembering what I had prayed, we walked into the house. I immediately saw the gorgeous view of the golf course, the openness of the layout, and the brightness of the incoming light from a full wall of windows, and said,

"Where do I sign?"

It was wonderful! It was almost twice the square footage of the California house; had a separate living area for Mom versus my bedroom area, so she could have her privacy, and it had a fenced yard for Cricket. It had tile throughout the house, which made it look lovely and very different from what we were used to; and the kitchen was huge. God had given me everything I could want in a house and more! We made a deal on the house before we left town that third day.

On the flight home, Mom and I talked about selling the California house. Remember the pain of the remodel?? That was just perfect too! It made our house immediately available to sell! A realtor had been bugging me about the opportunity to list my house for the past year, and had stopped multiple times during our remodel. My answer had been consistently, "No! I'm never selling after what we've been through on this remodel!" Silly me!

Mom and I agreed this was the right realtor to sell my house. I called him on Sunday afternoon about the opportunity; he came over within the hour. When I suggested the price for listing the house, he asked would it be acceptable if he got me more money than that? I laughed and naturally agreed. The house was to list the next day, but our realtor had a buyer for us that night! Amazing! It was another "God-thing" as my friend, Sally, would say!!

In the excitement of the opportunity I actually hadn't worked out the details of the job offer with Fran yet, but I was convinced it would be acceptable the way everything was falling into place. It started as a sales job, which later turned into an operations management job … but the good news was it provided a living and benefits for the next 5 ½ years! The Lord was so good to Mom and me again.

At this point, Mom said, "When God's in it, you'd better have roller skates on!" I never agreed with her more!

That was literally how fast this opportunity became a reality! We were going to be "moving on" to Texas within the next month, after my living in the California house for 48 years!

Mom and I had a lot to do to get ready for our next "adventure," and together we set about making it happen.

*　　*　　*　　*　　*

What's Next? ...

When Mom was selling her Florida condo, people commented to her, "Wouldn't it be funny if you went all the way to California, and then some day ended up moving back to Florida?"

Mom responded, "It wouldn't surprise me! I know God has a good sense of humor!"

*   *   *   *   *

In Dallas, we'd be halfway back to Florida!

Little did we know what lay ahead for us.

But here we were positioned to be "Coming Full Circle!"

Chapter 7

COMING FULL CIRCLE

"I can do all things through Christ,
who strengtheneth me."
Philippians 4:13

I had missed many blessings earlier in my life by not obeying the Lord's direction sooner. When this Texas employment opportunity became a reality so quickly, delaying to obey God's leading was not an option from my perspective. No one was more supportive than Mom. No one was more shocked by it all than me. No one could make it all come together as planned, but the Lord.

I had started getting acquainted with my sales job for Fran's company remotely because I was to start work the day after we arrived in Texas.

> My "cheerleader" Mom gave me a card showing the back end of a turtle on the front, and inside it said: "Behind you all the way!" She wrote, "You are going to be a great salesperson - if I could do it - so can you! Both Cricket and I know you will be the top producer in '04! Love, Mom."

I really appreciated her encouragement because at some points of this new adventure doubts crept in. I had to push them away believing the Lord had put together this plan; we just needed to carry it out!

We were moving to a larger home, so all our furniture could transfer. Carl flew out to California to drive "Big Red II" to its next destination, Farmers Branch, Texas! A friend built a platform for the Cadillac's backseat, about 1" thick and covered with carpeting - for the longest R-I-D-E of Cricket's life! We hired a mover and packed it all up; said goodbye to family, friends, and neighbors; and headed to Texas - all within about four weeks of the house sale!

Life in Texas ...

We stayed in a nearby hotel until the furniture arrived. It was fortunate Mom was so experienced and capable to orchestrate the unpacking because I went to work immediately.

Cricket fell in love with her new view of the world. A wrought iron fence enclosed the backyard, so virtually nothing blocked her view. Cricket's California view had been limited to what could be seen from our front door between two bushes. Now she could see squirrels, rabbits, and birds on the golf course; she watched golfers in carts driving by or those who managed to hit balls in our yard and thought they could retrieve them; and she had spacious, lovely scenery to view. Later I would learn that an occasional coyote would wander through the golf course early on the cool mornings looking for breakfast! I told Cricket she had to come in the house when that happened because she'd look like a "buffet table offering," to a skinny, hungry coyote!!

We found a church nearby that was within driving distance, so Mom would be comfortable going to services there if work kept me from attending with her. Pastor Hays and his excellent preaching, the friendly congregation, and the cheerful music at Valwood Park Baptist Church let us know it was the church for us to attend. After only two weeks, we became members! We really enjoyed the fellowship there and many became our close friends.

It wasn't too long before Mom and I were involved with numerous Mission Committee projects that were scheduled almost bi-monthly.

Mom joined the other seniors who cleaned the sanctuary every Friday morning which reduced church cleaning costs. She was very happy to serve the Lord in this task; I think she primarily enjoyed the fellowship with other seniors!

Mom and I even made our "acting debut" at Valwood Park Baptist during their annual Variety Show. Mom played a 'Prissy Presbyterian' and I played a 'Bratty Baptist' in a skit we wrote entitled "The First Time Visitor." Everyone laughed a lot so they must have enjoyed it, including Mom and me having the fun of creating it!

It didn't take people long to get to know what a special person Mom was. An exercise in our Sunday School class was to write a comment anonymously about each member, by completing the phrase: "This is what I have learned to appreciate about you_____" One comment about Mom was: "She is generous, faithful, strong in her faith, and a mover behind the scenes. She makes things happen and doesn't look for glory." Another said she's: "A very giving person; she sees a need and does something about it without any thought of praise or reward; she's totally honest and true to her word; a loyal, dependable friend; she loves others with the love of Christ." Others had many nice things to say about Mom, but I only selected these two to share. Mom felt she wasn't doing anything worthwhile for the Lord; yet look what shone through in Mom's words and deeds!

We also joined the Country Club affiliated with the golf course on which our property bordered. We'd have brunch each Sunday at the Club after attending church. Mom had missed this aspect of Cove Cay when she moved to California, so really enjoyed the Country Club association in our new location.

We found a nice coffee shop around the corner from our house and would start our day together, before I left for work, with a good breakfast out. Guess who could R-I-D-E along and then wouldn't bug Grandma all day for one? Yes, Cricket looked forward to that outing ... and Mom always saved a little bite of her breakfast for "Ms. C" as she lovingly called her.

It didn't take long to learn that Texas had some radical weather!! Two weeks after we moved there, it snowed about 2"! I had asked Fran about snow, and she told me it rarely snowed! I thought it was pretty early for a "rare" snowstorm!! But when I called her, she told me to take a photo quickly because it would melt by mid-afternoon, and she was absolutely correct!

I thought Florida had extreme thunder and lightning storms ... but the wide-open spaces of Texas seemed to allow some crazy winds to blow through with an even bigger version of thunder and lightning! We frequently heard tornado warnings going off! Fortunately, during our time there, only once did we hear the "sound of a train" coming down the golf course - to learn the next day a tornado had come through that night. The many trees down were proof of that!

Poor Cricket was terribly afraid of the thunder and lightning! The problem was she would try to squeeze between some furniture for protection near Mom or me - in a space about 4" wide for a dog that was about 10" wide!! Made for some interesting moments as we had to catch the falling pieces of furniture!!

For our 8th Mother's Day, we enjoyed our first rodeo together! Ya-hoo!! On other occasions, we also attended Ranger baseball and Cowboy football games. Mom was quite the avid fan, whether in front of the TV or at an actual event!

My cousins and great-aunt lived about a one-hour drive away from us and allowed for some family get-togethers. My nieces came to visit for a week in the summer.

Mom attended a San Diego work conference with me; we were happy to see some of our California friends while in the vicinity. Shortly after this trip, Fran sold the company to another industry competitor and retired to Clearwater, Florida. The new company had great plans for our products and we were excited by the prospects of more growth.

Mom's Lengthy Gout Battle ...

It was fortunate that we got active as soon as we moved to Texas, because starting in late 2004 some health issues hampered Mom's lifestyle ... and would seriously impact her going forward.

Mom was diagnosed with gout, which was very painful in her feet and toes. The gout worsened due to kidney problems, caused by certain prescribed medicines she had been taking. Unfortunately, she was allergic to the traditional gout medicines and the bad reactions to those drugs took a further toll on her health.

Most of the time she wasn't even able to wear shoes. The pain and swelling worsened from poor circulation as a result of her two knee surgeries. Sadly, Mom had to sit in a recliner lift chair much of the time to help reduce the swelling by elevating her feet. She had the same lovely view that Cricket enjoyed. But, as active as Mom had been, it was tough to scale back that much. Her mind was still very good, but her body began weakening.

We even took a trip to Mayo Clinic in Minnesota in the dead of winter to see if they could help Mom. Flip-flops were the only footwear Mom could tolerate during this freezing trip. I thought she was going to deck a well-meaning lady at the Minnesota airport who suggested Mom should consider wearing warmer footwear in this blizzard type weather! If Mom could have, she would have! That incident made me a little more sensitive about suggesting things to people who may have health issues preventing what I might thoughtlessly be suggesting.

But even Mayo couldn't help Mom with any new remedies for her gout. They told us a new medicine was in the Food and Drug Administration's (FDA) testing stage but until it was released, there was absolutely no way she could get that drug for relief.

Fortunately, we kept looking for a doctor who would help Mom and came across a very special Internist, Dr. Steve Lau in Dallas, who took extra interest in Mom's case. His earnest research located a drug that had been around for decades that worked specifically on reducing the Uric Acid; but the medicine was now only available through Canada. So, that's the route Mom went until the newly developed medicine passed the FDA testing (which wouldn't occur for three more years).

In spite of the pain, suffering, and limitations in Mom's life from this chronic gout problem, she never complained. Her philosophy was: "I have a choice to make it a good day or not ... and I choose to enjoy each one!" She did just that, finding ways to connect with people from her chair, by phone, letter, or other kind deed. We called it her "ministry from the footstool."

As her health issues increased, Mom was wise and brave enough to tell me, "You may want to promise that you'll never put me in an assisted care facility, J'Gay. But it might be needed. If so, Sweetheart, I'll understand and trust you to make the right decision."

I assured Mom that we would keep her home as long as possible, as long as we could provide proper care for her and could afford to provide the 24 hour care that could be needed at some point.

What a "gift" a parent could give their family members by admitting that might be a possibility and helping to ease the struggle of that tough decision on another's behalf. How unselfish of Mom ... and just like her ... to give me permission to make that decision if ever needed! I silently prayed I would never have to make that choice.

In addition to her walker, Mom was using an electric cart to get around better ... and our Texas home looked like it had been designed to accommodate that kind of aid. The tile throughout the house made it easier for Mom to maneuver. (Again, God knew what was needed before we got there! Even the remodel at the California house would not have allowed for her maneuvering with an electric cart.)

The gout had caused Mom to no longer be able to drive "Big Red II." She said she had wondered if she'd know when to quit driving and have the good sense to stop. The decision was an obvious one for her, although one of the tougher ones to accept. Mom missed the independence the ability to drive allowed, and wasn't happy about the additional dependence on me that required.

Mom's 80th Birthday Celebration ...

In November 2005, Carol and I hosted Mom's 80th Birthday Party at the Country Club. Fifty friends including several from Florida helped her celebrate!

We had balloons and decorations all over the house that made Mom smile.

Carol and I gave Mom an Alaskan Cruise as her gift, which the three of us got to enjoy!

When we booked the Alaska Cruise, we knew the cruise line could accommodate Mom's electric cart. It was wonderful that Mom didn't object to using whatever means helped her continue to be mobile. My stepmother was too proud to even use a cane or walker, and missed out on so much of life. But not Mom ... she wanted to keep going and doing as long as God allowed it! I hope I remember this lesson when I need it!

In Mom's thank you note to me for the party, she wrote, "Thank you for all the planning (especially at your busy time). You child are something else and I love you more now then ever before. I am so proud of what you have done with your life! I hope my genes had something to do with your many successes! You are a terrific kid! Love, Mom"

It still felt very good that she loved me so much and didn't mind telling me.

2006 Good Memories ...

We celebrated our 9th Reunion Anniversary on February 9th.

In my card to Mom, I wrote: "Thanks, Mom, for the past 9 years together. I've really learned to enjoy life in totally different ways by your love, support, and encouragement. What a terrific blessing to have "Mama Bear" in my corner - praying for me, easing my life each day in every way, and loving me no matter what! At least I don't wake up daily wondering if your love will last - I KNOW it's ALWAYS there! Please KNOW mine is there for you FOREVER too, by God's plan! Love and Happy Anniversary, J'Gay"

For Mother's Day, Mom accompanied me to a Partner Conference in Nashville, Tennessee. Thanks to an electric cart we rented from the hotel, she was able to be very mobile. She thoroughly and safely enjoyed herself while I had to work and she needed to maneuver around on her own.

We were able to see the Grand Old Opry and take a dinner cruise on board the General Jackson Showboat, making new memories for both of us.

2006 Not-So-Good Memories ...

This was the year of health issues for both of us.

I had to have knee surgery for a torn meniscus in August. What I thought would be a four-day recovery turned into six weeks on crutches! The doctor tried to repair it instead of remove the torn part. That required my working remotely in order to put no weight on it at all.

In November, Mom went into renal failure from a bad reaction to an antibiotic for a Urinary Tract Infection. She had to be hospitalized and ended up in the Intensive Care Unit (ICU). She was close to not making it through this crisis. Carol flew out from Florida as Mom's health worsened. Dialysis was required at one point. I was very worried Mom wasn't going to make it. What a helpless feeling to watch someone you love dying.

I was sitting in the Waiting Area with a few other friends when the Hospital Chaplain stopped by to see us. He said a prayer and gave a pamphlet to each of us. When I looked at mine, I was instantly encouraged and knew Mom was going to make a "comeback." The Scripture on my pamphlet was Psalm 121! The other ladies had Psalm 23 imprinted on theirs. I knew this was no coincidence! Psalm 121 was the Scripture that God spoke to Mom after I had been kidnapped from her when she thought she was going to lose her mind. It gave her great peace then - it did the same for me that day! A note from the

Lord of Heaven assuring me it would be all right, whatever way it turned out.

Two days later, Mom looked at me and said: "Janet Gayle, what are you doing to get me out of here??" Normally I would think she was kidding! But when she uses "Janet" and "Gayle" ... it's serious! She didn't understand why I wasn't doing something to get her out of ICU, which was certainly something I wanted to happen!

Four days later, Mom was home recovering her strength from her ordeal. Her "comeback" was slow however. When you almost die, I think there's a big shock to your system that requires time to heal. We had home health caregivers lined up to assist. Her "comeback" would take over two years.

About two weeks later, my knee gave out again and required another surgery! The initial repair didn't hold. They had to go in and remove the tear or fix it ... whatever they do. But I was laid up a few more weeks. So, we both had home health caregivers until I was able to function independently again!

Then, Mom was additionally diagnosed with spinal stenosis, a painful compression in her back, that required the home caregivers to continue when I had to return to work.

One of Mom's biggest regrets was she had to stop being part of the volunteer senior cleaning team at church on Friday mornings! She just couldn't have her feet down long enough to even clean for a few hours.

On Sunday afternoon as I tucked her in for a nap after church, Mom would tell me that God answered her prayer one more time. He gave her the strength to go to church that morning. How many people never go to church who have the energy to do so every week? And Mom was making it a matter of special prayer to just have the strength to attend one more time! Wow ... did that ever teach me another lesson in priorities!

Special Events of 2007 ...
Two special events occurred for us in February 2007.

Mom and I celebrated our 10th Reunion Anniversary on February 9th! What a great decade it had been. We packed lots of living into those 10 years. Both of us prayed we could have more years, and for Mom to have another pain-free season, Lord willing. We cherished each day the Lord gave us and realized we'd have FOREVER together, no matter what!

Mom flew Carol out for my 60th birthday later in February! Mom was so excited to be able to plan and execute the surprises she had planned for me.

She had some trouble convincing a local limousine company that she wanted a stretch limo for the evening for just the three of us! They kept telling her a Lincoln Towncar would suffice and be less costly. Guess who won?! We ate at a mystery dinner theatre and the stretch limo waited to take us home!

Work and Health Issues Increase ...

2007 was a very rough year-end at the new company.

I was transferred into an Operations Manager position, which was through another miracle in my life! Someone I had helped some 25 years earlier in their career was in a position at this new company to remember me and recalled what my background had been. He actually recommended me for the Operations role versus being laid-off as originally planned! Another good lesson in life: do your best every chance you get; someone might be watching who could be in a position later to bless you in return!

By the way, Sales wasn't my forte as it was Mom's. I was better suited to Operations management and enjoyed it more - but Mom's encouragement followed me in whatever career path I was pursuing. That I could count on!

The Operations Manager job began requiring many hours again, as the Payroll Tax business tends to do. I didn't think I would physically be able to give that many hours at this point of life, but I did the best I could to meet all of the job demands.

I was trying to spend what time I could with Mom. I missed our breakfasts together, because she was in too much pain to go out to breakfast and too weary to have breakfast at home together before I went to work. The two shifts of day caregivers were a big help while I worked the extra hours. I provided the night shift home health care coverage for Mom.

Mom's health continued to decline. She couldn't sit, stand, or lay comfortably as the back pain increased tremendously. She kept worrying about taking too much pain medicine; she "didn't want to become an addict." But she needed it to keep functioning as well as she could. Every time I'd get her to believe it was acceptable to take the pain medicine as prescribed by her doctor, due to her severe gout and back pain, something would show on TV about that medicine causing drug addiction! I finally had to play the "age card" and say, "Mom, you're 82 years old; it's okay if you have this addiction because it helps keep your pain under control!"

But we never stopped "shopping" for better solutions for Mom's health issues. In 2008, Mom chose to have back surgery, as the surgeon felt he could alleviate her pain to a certain degree. Gout contributed much toward her severe back pain and complicated the original surgery. However, a secondary complication required her to have a subsequent surgery. That led to considerable recovery time at a rehabilitation facility (rehab) near our house.

I couldn't have gotten through this latest crisis without Carol's help. She flew in from Florida once again to help. I would be with Mom before and after work; Carol would visit with Mom during the day. The thoughtful, caring people from our church would also make sure Mom had a visitor at least once a day to cheer her up and pray with her.

As Mom's rehab stay extended to several weeks, more lessons were learned about those who reside in a rehab facility and have no friends, no visitors, no mail ... and not much hope, except that one of the workers will get them to the table for their next meal. What an eye-opener this was for me about the numerous people who are afflicted like this. Our Valwood Park Baptist Church's Mission Committee actually sponsored some projects to raise funds to make activities and prizes available for these residents in two of the area rehab facilities as a result of these life lessons!

Thank God each day you can get up under your own power, get dressed, feed yourself, and enjoy some portions of life ... while you still can! And may God bless those workers called to serve in rehab facilities to assist those who can't do for themselves any longer! It was truly a side of life I would not have seen, nor comprehended, if I hadn't witnessed it during Mom's recovery process.

Finally, Mom got strong enough to come home ... but not before she called me one day and told me her "roommate was behind her kidnapping!" That I'd "better come help" her because she was being held against her will!

I said I'd "be there in 20 minutes!" I prayed fast and fervently: "Please God, don't let her be losing her mind too at this point!" I didn't think I could handle that and her failing health too.

When weekend personnel replaced the regular staff, Mom had gotten confused and alarmed by the new faces. I clarified that for Mom, spoke with her doctor about her possibly being given too much pain medicine - and brought her home as soon as possible!

Mom's back pain lessened from the eventual success of the surgery. She was very brave to go through that procedure and what it took to "graduate" from rehab to be able to come home again! With the help of pain medicines, and finally the release of the new gout drug to the marketplace, which Mom could tolerate, Mom started to improve once again. That was very encouraging, and most welcome!!

Life started to move towards normal again. But we didn't get to bask in that "sunshiny" position for long!

More Unexpected Life Changes ...

My employer was sold again to another industry competitor, which we were led to believe would provide a high growth opportunity for our division. Unfortunately, in May 2009, our division was subjected to a sizeable layoff ... and I was one of those staff reductions.

The layoff came the day after Mom and I had returned from a one-week Florida vacation. During that vacation, my friend, Fran, asked if I ever thought about retiring to Florida. I said I hadn't given it much thought but it didn't sound like a bad idea. Mom was surprised and pleased by that prospect. I was actually surprised by my answer as well!

As you might have guessed, this was a very timely topic for discussion. When the layoff occurred within the next two days, I knew the Lord had planted that Florida retirement "seed" as our possible next step. It only took me 24 hours to weigh our options, calculate a retirement budget, and discuss the relocation to Florida with Mom as our #1 logical choice. Not only was it a good budgetary alternative, but Mom would also be near her old friends and other family again. She had received a very warm welcome from everyone we had seen during that Florida vacation.

Mom was in total agreement about the retirement move. Terrific supporter that she was, Mom had never told me she missed Florida and would like to go back some day. Mom knew if I knew she wanted to go back, I would have done all in my power to make that happen ... just to make sure she was happy. By waiting, we were now both enthused with the prospect of a Florida-relocation.

God had allowed one "complication" to be removed just before we left on that Florida vacation. Cricket's back and hind legs had given out on her, and I had to make the difficult decision to have the vet put her down; he came to the house and I held Cricket in my lap until the end. I don't think I stopped crying for a whole week, Mom neither. But I had no doubt it was the right decision. Life at the house was so different without our Cricket. I had her for 12 ½ years, mostly on "borrowed time" when the vet had told me at 6 weeks she wouldn't make it without surgery. Mom had been able to enjoy her "grandkid" for about 7 years; and Mom's life had definitely been enriched by spending time with Cricket, and vice versa.

With no pet to consider in our move, that opened the possibility of moving into a condominium and making our lives simpler than caring for a home in our later years. So, we contacted Mom's realtor, Kathy in Florida; worked with her on the phone and by email; and selected some condos to see during an exploratory visit.

Meanwhile, we put our Texas house on the market with Trish. We began the downsizing task and started packing up our goods to be ready to move whenever the house sold. Based on our California selling experience, I was preparing for this Texas move at a rapid pace.

We headed off to Florida for a quick trip to view properties. Amazingly, Kathy showed us a 3-bedroom condo available that we just loved. It happened to be in the building next to the one Mom and Dad had lived in at Cove Cay when I located Mom 12 years earlier. Since living at Cove Cay had been such a pleasant experience for Mom, and was a very nice experience during my visits to see Mom and Dad, we had no reservations about buying that condo. Mom would be able to get around readily in her electric scooter, much better than she was able to in our Texas house. While we toured the Cove Cay properties again, Mom received a very warm welcome from many of the residents who knew her there before her California move. We made the condo offer before we headed back to Texas.

When we returned to Texas, however, God seemed to have other plans for us! All of a sudden from the pressures of work, extra strain of caring for my 80-pound "kid," Cricket, during her final few weeks, and the stress of our move preparations, my back and upper right shoulder froze up. They were so painful I couldn't even sit at the computer for five minutes to view emails. So, I went to the chiropractor and had therapy for the next few months.

Mom needed the time to recover her strength as well. The two Florida trips in the short timeframe, plus the excitement of the prospective move, had her extra tired.

So, again God knew best for us, and the Texas house stayed on the market for five long months! We re-thought our decision to move, but still concluded we were doing what God had led us to do - we just hadn't figured out His timetable yet for this move!

After what it took for God to get my attention previously, I was really trying to wait patiently for His timing - it was painful not to listen!

Our Move to Florida ...

It was a tough season for Texas real estate, as it was nationwide. Other homes in our neighborhood that had gone on the market before ours were still not sold; many were making great financial concessions to sell. Our condo in Florida was closing rapidly - and we really needed to get the Texas house sold at our asking price! Lots of prayers finally moved God's hand. We accepted an offer on the house with a modest concession, which was offset by the savings on the Florida condo deal. So, we knew God's timing was finally right - for Him and us!

By the way, if I never participate in another Open House, or put out another Open House sign in my lifetime, that would make me very happy! Another occupation experienced and better left to those called into it! It did give me some appreciation of Mom and Dad's real estate careers.

Meanwhile, I filed for Social Security and officially retired. Mom and I were really looking forward to spending more time together, experiencing some new things in Florida, and enjoying the Cove Cay lifestyle!

It was hard to say good-bye to the friends we had made in the Dallas area during our 5 ½ years there. But it was time to move on again; and we did so without looking back. All had an open invitation to come see us in Florida, or we'd make plans to see them again during any stopover visit on another trip we might take. That thinking made leaving a little easier.

We moved into our Cove Cay condo in late October 2009. We enjoyed being nearer to Carol and Carl again, and nearer to Mom's godson, Andrew, and family too. We had Thanksgiving together with several of our Florida "family." We were also able to participate in the Cove Cay holiday potluck at the little clubhouse.

Before we had left Dallas, part of our downsizing was to give away the majority of our cold weather clothing. Mom told me that we wouldn't need them in the warm winters of Florida. That turned out not to be the case as Florida experienced its coldest winter in many decades! Naturally, we were blamed for that unique experience being the outsiders, like we had caused the snowstorm in Dallas as soon as we had arrived! We actually had to shop for some warmer clothes again to survive the cold Florida weather - and remember, poor Mom was still in her flip-flops!

We attended Lakeview Baptist Church in Clearwater about the second Sunday we were settled in our condo, and joined that friendly church the second week we attended. We knew that was where the Lord wanted us; we had been praying about it for almost six months!

I could tell Mom was delighted to be back! She kept asking me if I was happy at Cove Cay and I assured her I was. I'd ask her the same question and she'd say, "Absolutely!" Together we knew "coming full circle" was a good thing for both of us.

Over the Christmas holiday, Mom and I went south to Sanibel Island for a three-day getaway. Mom had special memories of time spent at this vacation spot and wanted me to share it with her. I thought perhaps we had found a new Christmas tradition! Mom was very tired that trip, but I thought it was because of the recent move and all the excitement leading up to it. So, we did a lot of resting, watched TV, and ate out; she continued to beat me at Gin Rummy!

Little did we know that would be our last trip together.

The Unexpected Happens ...

I took Mom to the doctor for her scheduled check-up in early January. She complained of being tired, but test results indicated no serious problems at that time.

On the night of January 14, Mom said she felt very weak and tired. She also told me she "missed Dad so much," which she rarely said. I could see she was struggling to just make it with her walker from the living room to the bathroom.

As I tucked her in that night, I told her, "I'm not sure what's wrong Mom, but if you're not feeling better in the morning, we'll take you back to the doctor. I'm with you all the way to find out what's going on."

She looked at me and said, "I know I'm dying, Honey." At which point I know I looked shocked by what she said! There was no masking that reaction! But she quickly assured me, "It's okay, Honey, it doesn't hurt. I'm just sad because I thought we'd have more time to do more things together."

Naturally, I had trouble controlling my tears at that point. But I figured for certain we would be taking her to the doctor in the morning with her talking like that! Again, I thought maybe her mind was going. I kissed her good night and told her, "I love you THIS MUCH!" She agreed, and quickly fell asleep.

About 5AM, on January 15, I heard Mom trying to get up to go to the bathroom. I jumped out of bed to try to assist her. But she was too weak to be able to get to her side potty chair and I couldn't help with her having no strength in her limbs. She sat down on the carpeted floor; she didn't fall, it was a graceful sitting down cross-legged. I explained to Mom that I needed to call the Paramedics and we'd see what the hospital learns about her weakness.

She was checked into the Emergency Room, where they discovered she had a serious Urinary Tract Infection. I quickly told them about the problem she'd previously had with a bad reaction to the certain family of antibiotic for treating that type of problem. They assured me they would prescribe something else.

She was checked into a room for a few days of treatment. The next day she was responding so well to the antibiotic, she even started eating the hospital food!

Carol and Carl started taking turns coming to sit with Mom while I took a daily lunch break. A friend from church, who had come to the Emergency Room to pray for Mom and me the previous day, came on this second day and couldn't believe how improved Mom was already.

That night I went home to sleep, though reluctant to leave Mom's bedside. She called me at 7AM the third day and asked when I was coming to see her. I said I was in the shower and would be there shortly.

That third day, January 17, I noticed she was having trouble breathing and mentioned it to some of the doctors on her treatment team, asking if they could check her for possible pneumonia. They said the pneumonia was beginning and would change her medicine to combat both problems. I explained again about her bad reaction to that certain antibiotic, and they assured me they would prescribe something else.

They brought in some oxygen and a breathing mask later that afternoon, to get some medicine into her lungs. She didn't handle the mask very well, due to being very claustrophobic, just like me, but I explained the purpose was to get some medicine into her lungs that would prevent the pneumonia from worsening.

She started asking when she could go home. One of the doctors explained she would likely have to go to a rehab facility first in order to recover her strength and get back on her feet. I could tell right away she wasn't happy about the prospect of rehab again. I explained she needed to be able to move around on her own or with some assistance and, until her limbs were strengthened, she couldn't be at home and risk falling again.

Either the prospect of rehab again, or the antibiotic change, caused Mom to start on a downward spiral.

As soon as the pneumonia started developing, I advised Carol and Carl of this change in Mom's health. They were willing to stay longer that day, but I told them I would spend the night to be sure she had help if needed. The nurses encouraged me to go home. But I didn't want to leave Mom alone. I asked Mom if she'd prefer that I sleep in the chair at the foot of her bed, and she nodded "Yes." After she got ill about six times that night, I knew I made the right decision to stay with her because the nurses wouldn't have been able to be as attentive as I was.

That night we had quite a few "dialogues" about her needing to keep the oxygen mask on so the medicine could work. I would look up at her, and she would be pulling the mask away from her face; I'd then tell her if that snapped back at her, she would have a broken nose too, so she needed to keep it on. At one point she removed the mask entirely and said, "So let's just not do this anymore." I quickly got up and explained it was her only hope to see if the medicine into her lungs would help. But the direction all this was going was not looking positive.

She tried again to have the mask on. So, I covered up with a blanket and closed my eyes, then looked over at her, and she was lifting up the mask again. The last time I looked at her and saw her lifting up the mask, she said, "Peek-a-boo!" and laughed because she got caught! We both laughed at that point. Sadly, I knew the mask was a losing battle.

The next morning, January 18, when the doctors arrived, they told me the results of her blood work. By this time, Mom was unable to speak anymore; she had gone into what I would describe as a "labored breathing sleep mode." Mom wasn't getting enough oxygen into her body and in effect was going into heart failure. The only choices were to keep the mask on 100% of the time or have some artificial help to breathe. I said, "No, the artificial help wasn't an option," according to her Medical Power of Attorney wishes. I also knew having the mask on 100% of the time would not work either and explained that to the doctors as well. I know Mom could hear what was going on, even though she couldn't speak. She kept waving her index finger at me like she wanted the oxygen-measuring device removed too, thinking it was artificially sustaining her.

So, I asked the doctors to make her as comfortable and pain-free as possible, but to discontinue treatment, which they set about doing immediately. The doctors told me she would not last very long.

This was shocking since we had seen Mom progressing so well just two days prior! I was heartbroken, but knew Mom … and the Lord … had made the choices clear to me.

I called Carl and Carol, explaining what was happening and how quickly it was happening. While I was making those calls out of the room, our pastor came by and prayed with Mom. When I returned to the room, Mom couldn't speak but was waving that index finger toward her tray on which I saw our pastor's business card. I said, "I see Pastor Link was here and must have prayed with you." She settled right down knowing I understood what she was trying to tell me. She didn't say another word, just went deeper into her peaceful sleep.

I also called the funeral home for an appointment to make Mom's final arrangements. When Carl and Carol arrived, I asked Carol if she'd go with me in a little while on that "errand," while Carl stayed with Mom.

Miracles Ease the Way …

We were sitting around Mom's beside, trying to keep the conversation as pleasant as possible. All of a sudden, Mom spoke and said two things: "There's Grandpa (which was her father and my grandfather, Joe)," and, "There's Bill (my step-dad)."

At that point, I said, "Mom, if they are there to greet you, you go on to Heaven. I don't want you to go, but it must be time for me to let you go. I'm so glad we had the time together we did and made the most of it. I will always love you THIS MUCH!"

No more was said by Mom; but I know she gave us a glimpse of her about to enter Heaven and being greeted by the two people she dearly loved and had hoped to see again.

(It wasn't lost on me that Dad had told me, just before he died, Mom and I "would have a good ten years to enjoy our lives together," and now he showed up to welcome her at that 10-year mark! Amazing! As much as he loved Mom, Dad probably didn't let God alone about that 10-year date!)

Carol and I went to the cemetery for our appointment. Before we met about the detailed arrangements, we drove over to locate Mom's gravesite. This cemetery does something really special: they carve old trees into the shapes of animals, rather than cutting down the tree entirely. I noticed one of the carvings was a 15' statue of a Grizzly Bear. I told Carol, "Wouldn't it be neat if that was the animal that was near Mom's grave, as much as she loved bears!" When we located Dad's headstone, guess what was about 20' from it?! Yep, a huge carved Grizzly Bear stands watch over Mom and Dad's particular section of the cemetery! Another message from the Lord, that He had prepared this for Mom - and for me to feel better about what was about to happen.

We made the arrangements and went back to the hospital. I called Carl from downstairs to see if there was any change in Mom's condition, and he said "No, why don't you have a sandwich or something from the cafeteria." I asked him to call if anything changed.

I was taking my last bite of sandwich when Carl's call came. We hurried back to her room, but Mom had already died. He said as soon as he hung up from calling me, she breathed her last. No one will ever convince me Mom didn't know exactly where Carol and I had been. It also seemed Mom wanted me to eat something before coming back to her room, and she didn't want me to see her breathe her last breath.

At least the last words I had spoken to Mom were from the one clear memory I had of her for the 45 years we had been apart: "I love you THIS MUCH!"

*   *   *   *   *   *

As sad and sudden as Mom's passing was for me, I knew we had done all we could for as long as we could. We had made the most of the time God allowed us to have together.

While 45 years had been "stolen" from us, God had never "lost" track of either of us.

It was no accident Mom survived the train wreck. It was no accident that the luggage carrier fell on my head. It was no accident that Dad met Mom and helped take care of her for 40+ years before we were reunited. It was no accident I survived my Cadillac running over me. It was no accident a Grizzly Bear was now guarding Mom's grave. It was no accident we came "full circle" back to Florida, so Mom could see Florida again and be buried right next to Dad where she wanted to be.

For me, it was time to grieve again, but this time for loss of a true mother's love - an unconditional love, that without her, I would never have understood. I feel sad, but I don't feel empty. Instead, I still feel "joy unspeakable" whenever I think of Mom's love for me.

My condo contains many mementoes of our times together: artwork from our trips, photo albums from each trip, charms from distant locations Mom added to my charm bracelet, family collectible glassware, photographs of Mom - all shared memories that remind me of her wherever I look. They don't make me sad because my memories of her are happy ones. But none of the memories or mementoes matter like the touch of Mom's love in my life and how it filled my heart completely … forever.

But I did find myself asking, "What am I doing in Florida?!" This was Mom's home, not mine. These were Mom's friends and family, not mine. But that was changing. After a period of mourning, I realized Florida was now my home and I needed to actively make it that - bloom where I'm planted! Mom's family and friends were now my family and friends. They lovingly include me in their lives, and I have another loving church family to call on when I need help or just a friend.

God had spent the past 13 years moving me around the country … moving me through sadness to joy, moving me from comfortable to more adventuresome, moving me from just existing to seeking to live for Him. I knew I had better look up and see what God had next for me.

This book was the next step in His leading.

I hope it helps someone else to know that God never "loses" track of us. Whatever is "stolen" can be restored and replenished … in abundance. But it all happens in God's timing and for His purposes.

You just have to be willing and available for God to use.

Chapter 8

LESSONS LEARNED

"And we know that all things work together for good to them that love God, to them who are the called according to his purpose." Romans 8:28

One focus of *"Stolen But Not Lost"* was the 45 years "stolen" from the lives of my birth mother and me through difficult circumstances. Equally highlighted was the miracle that God never "lost" track of us during those missing years!

Within this book, I mentioned several "lessons learned" along the journey. However, there were five lessons in particular that focused on what was F-O-U-N-D as a result of our lifetimes of losses and eventual recovery. Those five lessons are ones I hope to never forget.

Perhaps one of these five "lessons learned" might help someone else with difficulties or uncertainties to overcome:

F – Find the truth

O – Open up to counseling

U – Uncover miracles available to you

N – Never think it's too late for dreams to come true

D - Don't delay to obey

Find the Truth

Remember there are two sides to every story, and be sure to get both sides before making any final decisions. Don't be too stubborn to learn the truth. It may not be what you want to hear, but hearing it will be worthwhile. It may take some time to deal with the truth or its results, but try to be open to it.

It's not our place to judge others; only God has a right to do that. It's easy to fall into that habit, but it tends to make a person close-minded. Making the judgment of right from wrong is our responsibility for our individual actions and thoughts; but shouldn't extend to our judging others if their right or wrong choices don't impact us.

When you learn the truth, some forgiveness may be needed. That might have to start with forgiving yourself. Others may be involved in the forgiveness to be extended as well. Don't let pride or stubbornness keep you bound by un-forgiveness.

Learning the truth may result in some disappointments. People or situations can be disappointing; your expectations may not be met. In this journey to find the truth about my birth mother and my life, several disappointments were part of that discovery process. A devotional from *"Our Daily Bread,"* (May 11, 1992) summarized it best for me:

"All that matters in the end is whether the disappointments of life pushed us into the arms of the Lord."

If you read *"Stolen But Not Lost,"* you know that is exactly what happened to me. As painful as the truth was, relying on the Lord and living life closer to Him was what the journey was all about.

The **most important truth** in life to learn, however, was not the main focus of this book. The **most important truth** is God's salvation message. There are two sides to this story too - one is choosing Eternal Life in Heaven, the other is choosing Hell forever.

I implore you to explore this truth and make the decision to accept God's free gift of Eternal Life. God offered this gift because He loves us so much He wants us to spend forever with Him. For us to be able to have that free gift, God gave His only Son, Jesus Christ, as the only acceptable sacrifice for our sins by Jesus' death on the cross.

To receive the gift of Eternal Life, each person only has to admit they have sinned or aren't perfect in God's eyes; believe that Jesus Christ died as the only acceptable sacrifice for their sin; confess that sin to God and ask Jesus Christ to be their personal Savior.

If you pray that prayer, as I have, I might not meet you here on earth. But God promised I will see you some day when we share Eternity together in Heaven with our Lord and Savior, Jesus Christ!

Please don't let doubt or untruth stand in your way.

Open Up to Counseling

Counseling gives you "someone in your corner." Your counselor takes a strong interest in helping you as their patient. They don't give you all the answers; they give you the opportunity to unearth the issues and work on the solutions from within yourself and for your particular situations.

If you don't want to keep the appointments or do the work assignments, or it's too painful to open up about difficult topics, the counselor cannot make you. But understand then that you won't be getting the full value of the counseling experience; those steps are designed to aid the healing process.

I can tell you the counseling process may hurt a lot. But if it does, I encourage you to persevere. If it hurts, it is needed. The results are worth the efforts. The only way you can get well is to be an active participant in the "getting well" process.

The pain of your past will need to be dealt with at some point in your life. Before those hurts cause anger too severe or depression too deep, my recommendation is for you to talk it out with a mental health professional or clergyman.

There is nothing wrong with admitting the pain is too great or complex for you to know how to handle it or where to begin to address it. Perhaps your insurance would even cover the costs of counseling sessions. It's worth checking out.

Another option is to journal your thoughts and feelings, like I did, to help sort them out and formulate a plan of action.

Just don't feel there is no hope or solution available to assist you. Admitting help is needed is half the battle! Being willing to work on the assignments, that might be required to work through the pain, is the other half to get you on the road to healing.

Uncover Miracles Available to You

I certainly believe in miracles! I'm living proof they can happen in ways you least expect it and at times you don't expect it.

Miracles may happen because you've asked for one or because you need one. If you're fortunate, you can even be part of someone else's miracle, which is a two-way blessing!

Sometimes people attribute a miracle to mere coincidence. A California Pastor, Ron Stevens, once explained that: "Coincidence is when God decides to do a miracle and still remains anonymous." Sometimes people don't recognize, or don't want to acknowledge, that perhaps a true miracle occurred.

The key, from my perspective, is to stay close enough to God to listen when He speaks. Then, be willing to act when He says to. You may need to be willing to go where He leads, to a place you didn't expect. So, being available is important. That opens you up to receive a miracle.

When a miracle occurs, be sure to thank God for it, even if it happens in a way other than you visualized or asked. From my experience, miracles happen in the way and in the timing God knew was best.

You may think you're no more significant than a grain of sand on the beach … but be assured: God owns that beach! He knows where, when, and how for each of us. We just need to be willing and available … and His miracles can abound in and through us!

Never Think It's Too Late for Dreams to Come True!

My dream started because I wanted to have a stronger testimony for the Lord. That started me on a road of life-changing events. Whatever you ask with a believing heart, just be prepared to accept the answer when it arrives!

My counselor told me it was "never too late for me to have my childhood." Then, she assigned the task of defining what that meant to me. If you can't define the goal, how do you know you've reached it?

My definition of "childhood" was: to laugh freely, be silly, enjoy life without worry, be more carefree. It meant to have few responsibilities at least for short periods of time; to explore new things; to exhibit freedom and spontaneity. It meant responding without fear of consequence.

The counselor then told me my next assignment was to "have fun!" I didn't even know where to start; but start I did! After work on a business trip, I bought a roll of quarters, found a pinball machine, and played at it until the money was gone! It was a small step, but it was a step forward! That was the start of realizing this dream I'd missed in my life. I was 46 years old before I started being a kid again! When "the bears would do funny scenes at night for my Mom to discover the next morning," that was all part of my being a kid and thoroughly enjoying it!

You have to define your own dreams. Then, plan how to achieve them. You need to see what you can do to still make them happen! Then, start executing those plans step-by-step. But the key is: you have to start!

Don't get discouraged if the plans don't work out at times or a step doesn't work in the process. Just don't abandon dreams if they really are important to you! Consider, however, that they might be easier to achieve if God is in them, so invite His participation and guidance.

Don't Delay to Obey

We only have today ... maybe only our next breath. So, we need to make the most of today with no guarantees of tomorrow.

If there is something that needs to be done, do it today. If there is something you want to pursue, don't delay in starting it. If there is something God wants you to do, by all means, don't delay to obey Him!

Don't require something to WHOMP you on the head, or require a car to run over you, for God to get your attention and you to "get the message," like I did! You need to be listening for His voice, and then be willing to obey ... without delay.

Don't be like me and miss many years of blessings by being too stubborn to listen and respond positively to God and His plans for your life.

Don't let the "What ifs" in life discourage you. Turn them into "All things!" as in:

"All things ... work together for good ...
according to his purpose." Romans 8:28

Consider what God might be trying to do in your life today. Be open to it and allow the Lord to richly bless your life!

* * * * *

Learning lessons can be easy or difficult ... but for sure, each one is worthwhile!

Chapter 9

SEARCH RESOURCES FOR MISSING PERSONS

Used in Search for Mom in 1997

NOTE:

>   Researching the Internet today is very different than in 1997.

>   There are undoubtedly many more organizations available to assist with adoption search requests.

>   Please be aware of possible Adoption search scams; be sure the organizations you choose are legitimate and come recommended based on their results or referrals they might provide.

The following represent some resources I used in 1997, and include some other search options based on their current availability on the Internet:

1. **Contact family members or old family friends** for information that might lead to clues on the whereabouts of the person you are seeking

2. **Access family birth certificates, marriage records, adoption papers,**

or death certificates for information about the individual being sought ... i.e. birth city and state, maiden names, possible family members, etc.

Write to: County Recorder, Vital Records, Dept of Health of City and State; request information or documents for name being sought; there may be a fee to obtain them

Note: Depending on the type of adoption, state laws and requirements may vary as to whether you would be able to obtain copies of the actual adoption papers.

3. **Send letter to: Social Security Administration (SSA)** requesting information about person being sought; and, if you want a letter forwarded to the party, include that with the request

SSA will search their records to locate the person; if they find a match, SSA will forward an inquiry and your letter to the person, and offer that person the option to respond to the inquiry or not

Include in the letter: as many details about missing person as known, such as Name of Person, Social Security # (if known), last known location; request the letter be forwarded to the party being sought; include check for the search services

Contact SSA for latest mailing address to be used, current fees charged, and other detailed questions you might have about this option

4. **Use people search engines on the Internet**, such as: www.whowhere. com or www.melissadata.com

5. **Use library Telephone Book White Pages** from the city and state where you believe the person was located

6. **Use a Search organization** such as: www.ussearch.com

(I don't find 1-800-U.S. Search, which I used, available by this name currently on the Internet; this may be a related search organization but I did not validate that.)

Please be aware that there are many scams on the Internet offering people and record search "teasers;" but all they produce are listings that could be located on various free websites by your own search efforts.

7. **Access www.adoption.org/adopt for various search options**

8. **Several adoption registry agencies exist;** some are dependent on both parties registering for their services in order for matches to be made.

Some of these sites are:
www.adopteeconnect.com
www.adoptiondatabase.org
www.registry.adoption.com
www.reunite.families.com
Birth Quest

9. ***Book available:*** "Lost and Found - The Adoption Experience"

10. **Write for CWLA's Guide to Adoption Agencies: A National Directory of Adoption Agencies and Adoption Resources from:**
Child Welfare League of America
440 First Street, NW Suite 310
Washington, DC 20001-2085

11. **Genealogy Discussion Groups** may have message boards or forums where people enjoy taking on the research challenge.

Some sites for these are:
http://boards.ancestry.com/
http://boards.rootsweb.com/
http://www.findagrave.com/forums/ubbthreads.php?ubb=postlist
&Board=58&page=1"

ACKNOWLEDGEMENTS

Special thanks to:

Beverly, my Family Counselor, without whom this journey to healing would not have been possible. Thanks for caring about me, Beverly, enough to keep pressing for the reunion at the right time. God bless you for the help you gave me through your special profession.

Sally, my dear friend and kind "editor" of this book. So often in this journey, I would have abandoned hope of the reunion if you didn't keep pressing on with other creative ways to continue the search! Your enthusiasm for the reunion process, and now with this book, was instrumental in both coming to fruition.

Linda, for the perfect book title. Thanks for listening, knowing what to say at the right time to encourage, and for praying for me.

All friends, mentioned by name or just remembered in my heart, for their role in this reunion process. Thank you for continuing to encourage me about the importance of writing this unique story.

Reunion Day 1997

Janet Tombow and mother, Norma Wallace